JUNIOR C\

LESS STRESS MORE SUCCESS

Maths Revision
Ordinary Level
Book 1
Number Strand and Algebra and Functions Strand

Brendan Guildea & Louise Boylan

g GILL EDUCATION

Gill Education
Hume Avenue
Park West
Dublin 12
www.gilleducation.ie

Gill Education is an imprint of M.H. Gill & Co.

978 07171 9070 6

Print origination: MPS Limited
Artwork: MPS Limited, Andriy Yankovskyy

For permission to reproduce photographs, the authors and publisher gratefully
acknowledge the following:
© Alamy: 133; © iStock/Getty Premium: vii, 42, 58, 59, 61, 71, 80, 86, 107, 109R, 117,
123, 130, 153, 156B, 169, 170, 172, 177; © Shutterstock: 88, 109L, 156T.

The authors and publisher have made every effort to trace all copyright holders. If,
however, any have been inadvertently overlooked we would be pleased to make the
necessary arrangement at the first opportunity.

Acknowledgements

The authors would like to thank Carol Guildea, Joe Heron and Jack Mahon who
helped with the proofreading, checked the answers and made valuable suggestions that
are included in the final text.

MIX
Paper from
responsible sources
FSC® C007507

CONTENTS

Please note:

The exam questions marked by the symbol 🔵 in this book are selected from the following:

1. SEC exam papers
2. Sample exam papers
3. Original and sourced exam-type questions

Introduction

The aim of this revision book is to help you get as high a mark as possible in your Junior Cycle Ordinary Level maths course. This book is designed to be exam focused and can be used in conjunction with **any** textbook.

Graded examples and exam questions

Throughout this book, **examples and exam questions are graded by level of difficulty**.

The level of difficulty is indicated by calculator symbols, as follows:

The number of calculators shown beside a question helps you know how difficult the question is. One calculator indicates a question which is relatively basic. As the questions get harder, the symbol will have more calculators. Three calculators will indicate an average-level question, whereas five calculators indicate that it is a very challenging question. These questions may be beyond some students, but give them a go! **Students hoping to achieve a high grade should aim to complete all of the 'five calculator' questions. The calculator symbol given for each question relates to the most difficult part of that question. Do not be discouraged by a challenging question.** In the Junior Cycle exam, difficult questions can sometimes begin with one or two simple parts; you should attempt as much as you can.

Preparing for your Junior Cycle maths exam

It is very important to realise that **you are your own best teacher**. Revision is when you begin to teach yourself. Thus, it is very important for you to start your revision as soon as possible. Make notes while you are revising. If you are having difficulty with a particular question, seek help from your teacher, a friend or a member of your family. As with all subjects, the best examination preparation is to work through past examination or sample papers so that you are familiar with the layout and style of questions.

So let's start at the beginning. If you want to do well in your Junior Cycle mathematics, then two things are essential:

- Revise effectively.
- Be familiar with the exam paper and so be prepared on the day of the exam.

These may seem obvious, but it's worth taking a moment to think about what these tips mean.

How to revise most effectively

If you are going to do well in the Junior Cycle, you are going to spend quite a bit of time revising. Spending a little time learning how to revise effectively will help you get more from your time and help you absorb and understand more of the material on the course. Here are some tips to help you revise for maths.

- Find a quiet place where you can work. This place should be dedicated to study, free of potential distractions. Turn off all music, the TV, computer and mobile phone.
- Draw up a study plan. Don't be afraid to ask your parents/teachers/guidance counsellor for help at this stage.
- Do the more challenging revision first, when you are fresh. Trying to focus on difficult problems when you are tired can be counter-productive.

Study in small chunks lasting 25 to 35 minutes. Your memory and concentration will work better if you study in short bursts, but often.

- Your maths course is based on understanding, so while you can 'learn' some elements of the course, it is important that you develop an understanding of the material.
- Drill and practice are essential ingredients for success in maths.
- Try to link any new material to things you know already. This is learning through association and helps long-term retention.

Don't get hung up on more difficult material. Concentrate on understanding the fundamental concepts and being able to answer all of the straightforward questions. Then, with time, you can build up to the more challenging problems.

Junior Cycle maths Assessment

Your assessment in Junior Cycle mathematics consists of four elements. We will look at these four elements in detail and in the order in which you will be completing them.

Classroom-Based Assessment 1 (CBA 1) – Mathematical Investigation (during second year)

Format: A report may be presented in a wide range of formats.

Preparation: A student will, over a three-week period in second year, follow the Problem-Solving Cycle to investigate a mathematical problem.

The Problem-Solving Cycle is as follows:

1. Define a problem
2. Decompose it into manageable parts and/or simplify it using appropriate assumptions
3. Translate the problem to mathematics, if necessary
4. Engage with the problem and solve it, if possible
5. Interpret any findings in the context of the original problem

5. Interpret findings

1. Define the problem

The Problem-Solving Cycle

4. Engage with and solve the problem

2. Break down the problem into parts

3. Translate the problem into maths

Assessment: The CBA is assessed by the class teacher.
A student will be awarded one of the following categories of achievement:

- Yet to meet expectations
- In line with expectations
- Above expectations
- Exceptional

Classroom-Based Assessment 2 (CBA 2) – Statistical Investigation (during third year)

Format: A report may be presented in a wide range of formats.

Preparation: A student will, over a three-week period in third year, follow the Statistical-Enquiry Cycle to investigate a mathematical problem.

The Statistical-Enquiry Cycle is as follows:

1. Formulate a question
2. Plan and collect unbiased, representative data
3. Organise and manage the data
4. Explore and analyse the data, using appropriate displays and numerical summaries
5. Answer the original question, giving reasons based on the analysis section

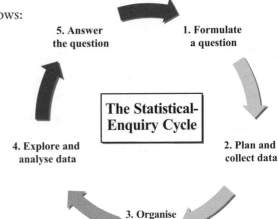

5. Answer the question

1. Formulate a question

The Statistical-Enquiry Cycle

4. Explore and analyse data

2. Plan and collect data

3. Organise and manage the data

Assessment: The CBA is assessed by the class teacher.
A student will be awarded one of the following categories of achievement:

- Yet to meet expectations
- In line with expectations
- Above expectations
- Exceptional

Assessment Task (during third year, after CBA 2)

Format: The Assessment Task is a specified written task, completed by students during class time.

Preparation: The Assessment Task is specified by the NCCA and is related to the learning outcomes on which CBA 2, the Statistical Investigation, is based.

Assessment: The Assessment Task is corrected by qualified teachers, as assigned by the SEC. The assessment task is allocated 10% of the marks used to determine the grade awarded by the SEC in Junior Cycle mathematics.

The written exam paper (end of third year)

Format: A two-hour written exam, taking place at the end of third year.

Assessment: The exam is corrected by qualified teachers, as assigned by the SEC. The written exam is allocated 90% of the marks used to determine the grade awarded by the SEC in Junior Cycle mathematics.

Read the exam paper right through at the start to determine which question is the easiest one to start with. Your mind may also be subconsciously processing some of the other problems.

Attempt marks are valuable, so it is vital that you attempt all questions.

Leave **NO** blanks.

Further exam tips

- There is no such thing as rough work in maths – all work is relevant. If the examiner doesn't know how you reached an answer, even a correct answer, then full marks will usually not be awarded. Thus, **show all your work**.
- It is a good idea to show each stage of a calculation when using a calculator (in case you press a wrong key). **Familiarise yourself with your calculator. Know your book of tables and formulae well and write down any formula that you use**.

Your calculator and book of tables are two extremely valuable resources to have in the exam. Make sure that you are very familiar with how your calculator works and that you know how to perform all functions on it. Also familiarise yourself with the book of tables so that you do not waste any time in the exam trying to find formulae.

- Attempt marks (partial credit) will be awarded for any step in the right direction. Therefore, **make an attempt at each part of the question**. Even if you do not get the correct answer, you can still pick up most of the marks on offer if you show how you worked it out. Also, **draw a diagram where possible**, because this can help you to see the solution.
- If you cannot finish part of a question, leave a space and come back to it later. **Never scribble out any work or use Tipp-Ex.** Put a single line through it so that the examiner can still read it. **Avoid using pencil** because the writing can be very faint and difficult to read.
- **Do not judge the length of your answer based on the size of the space provided.** Sometimes large spaces are provided for questions where only a short solution is required.
- If you run out of space in your answer booklet, **ask the supervisor for more paper**. Then clearly write the number of the exam question and the solution on the extra paper.

Glossary of common phrases used throughout your mathematics course and on the examination paper

Analyse, Investigate
Observe, study or examine something in detail, in order to establish facts and reach new conclusions.

Apply, Use
Select and use knowledge, skills or rules to put theory into practice and solve a problem.

Calculate, Find, Determine
Obtain your answers by showing all relevant work. Marks are available for showing the steps leading to your final answer or conclusion.

Classify
Group things based on common characteristics.

Comment on, Discuss, Interpret
After studying the given information or your answers, give your opinion on their significance. Use your knowledge and understanding to explain the meaning of something in context.

Compare
Give an account of the similarities and (or) differences between two (or more) items or situations, referring to both (all) of them throughout.

Construct
Draw an accurate diagram, usually labelled, using a pencil, ruler, set square, compass and protractor. Leave all constructions on your diagram.

Convert
Change from one form to another.

Estimate
State or calculate a rough value for a particular quantity.

Evaluate
Usually to work out, or find, a numerical value by putting in numbers for letters.

Explain, Show that, Prove, Verify, Justify
Demonstrate that a statement is true. This could be a given statement or to be able to show that your answer is correct.

Give your answer in the form ...
This means the examiner wants the final answer in a particular form, for example, as a fraction, in surd form, in index notation, rounded to a particular number of decimal places, etc. Watch out for this, as your will lose marks if your answer is not in the correct form.

Generalise
Generate a general statement, based on specific instance.

Generate
To produce or create.

Hence
You *must* use the answer, or result, from the previous part of the question.

Hence or otherwise
It is recommended that you use the answer, or result, from the previous part of the question, but other methods are acceptable.

Mathematise
Generate a mathematical representation (e.g. graph, equation, geometric figure) to describe a particular aspect of a phenomenon.

Plot
Indicate the position of points on a graph, usually on the x- and y-planes.

Sketch
Make a rough diagram or graph, labelled if needed.

Solve
Find the solution, or root, of an equation. The solution is the value of the variable that makes the left-hand side balance with the right-hand side.

Understand
Have detailed knowledge of, be able to use appropriately, and see the connections between parts.

Write down, State
You can write down your answer without showing any work. However, if you want you can show some workings.

Syllabus checklist for Junior Cycle Ordinary Level maths: Number Strand and Algebra and Functions Strand

Throughout your course you will be asked to apply your knowledge and skills to solve problems in familiar and unfamiliar contexts. In problem-solving, you should use some of the following strategies:

- Trial and improvement
- Draw a diagram
- Look for a pattern
- Act it out
- Draw a table
- Simplify the problem
- Use an equation
- Work backwards
- Eliminate possibilities

Unifying strand

Throughout the Junior Cycle maths course, students should develop the skills associated with each of the following elements:

Building blocks

Students should understand and recall the concepts that underpin each strand, and be able to carry out the resulting procedures accurately, effectively, and appropriately.

Representation

Students should be able to represent a mathematical situation in a variety of different ways and translate flexibly between them.

Connections

Students should be able to make connections within strands and between strands, as well as connections between mathematics and the real world.

Problem-solving

Students should be able to investigate patterns, formulate conjectures, and engage in tasks in which the solution is not immediately obvious, in familiar and unfamiliar contexts.

Generalisation and proof

Students should be able to move from specific instances to general mathematical statements, and to present and evaluate mathematical arguments and proofs.

Communication

Students should be able to communicate mathematics effectively in verbal and written form.

Number systems

- ☐ Understand the different types of numbers
    - ○ $\mathbb{N}$: the set of natural numbers $\{1, 2, 3, 4 \ldots\}$
    - ○ $\mathbb{Z}$: the set of integers, including 0
    - ○ $\mathbb{Q}$: the set of rational numbers
    - ○ $\mathbb{R}$: the set of real numbers
- ☐ Represent the operations of addition, subtraction, multiplication, and division in $\mathbb{N}$, $\mathbb{Z}$, and $\mathbb{Q}$ using models including the number line, decomposition, and accumulating groups of equal size.
- ☐ Perform the operations of addition, subtraction, multiplication, and division and understand the relationship between these operations and the properties: commutative, associative and distributive in $\mathbb{N}$, $\mathbb{Z}$, and $\mathbb{Q}$.
- ☐ Calculate and interpret factors (including the highest common factor), multiples (including the lowest common multiple), and prime numbers.

☐ Present numerical answers to the degree of accuracy specified, for example, correct to the nearest hundred, to two decimal places, or to three significant figures.

☐ Flexibly convert between fractions, decimals, and percentages.

Expressions

☐ Investigate situations in which letters stand for quantities that are variable.

☐ Generate and interpret expressions in which letters stand for numbers.

☐ Find the value of expressions given the value of the variables.

☐ Use the concept of equality to generate and interpret equations.

☐ Add, subtract and simplify:

○ linear expressions in one or more variables with coefficients in $\mathbb{Q}$

○ quadratic expressions in one variable with coefficients in $\mathbb{Z}$

☐ Multiply expressions of the form:

○ $a(bx + cy + d)$; $a(bx^2 + cx + d)$

○ $ax(bx^2 + cx + d)$, where $a, b, c, d \in \mathbb{Z}$

○ $(ax + b)(cx + d)$

☐ Divide quadratic by linear expressions, where all coefficients are integers and there is no remainder.

☐ Flexibly convert between the factorised and expanded forms of algebraic expressions of the form:

○ axy, where $a \in \mathbb{Z}$

○ $axy + byz$, where $a, b \in \mathbb{Z}$

○ $sx - ty + tx - sy$, where $s, t \in \mathbb{Z}$

○ $dx^2 + bx$

○ $x^2 + bx + c$

○ $x^2 - a^2$ where $a \in \mathbb{Z}$

Equations and inequalities

☐ Select and use suitable strategies (graphic, numeric, algebraic, trial and improvement, working backwards) for finding solutions to:

○ linear equations in one variable with coefficients in $\mathbb{Q}$ and solutions in $\mathbb{Z}$

○ quadratic equations in one variable with coefficients and solutions in $\mathbb{Z}$

○ simultaneous linear equations in two variables with coefficients and solutions in $\mathbb{Z}$

○ linear inequalities in one variable of the form $g(x) < k$, and graph the solution sets on the number line for $x \in \mathbb{N}, \mathbb{Z}$, and $\mathbb{R}$

Indices

- ☐ Flexibly translate between whole numbers and index representation of numbers.
- ☐ Use and apply rules for indices.
- ☐ Understand binary operations of addition, subtraction, multiplication and division in the context of numbers in index form.
- ☐ Correctly use the order of arithmetic and index operations including the use of brackets.
- ☐ Generalise numerical relationships involving operations involving numbers written in index form.
- ☐ Operate on the set of irrational numbers $\mathbb{R}\backslash\mathbb{Q}$.
- ☐ Convert the number p in decimal form to the form $a \times 10^n$, where $1 \leq a < 10$, $n \in \mathbb{Z}, p \in \mathbb{Q}$, and $p \geq 1$.

Patterns

- ☐ Analyse numerical patterns in different ways, including making out tables and graphs, and continue such patterns.
- ☐ Investigate patterns and relationships (linear, quadratic, doubling and tripling) in number, spatial patterns and real-world phenomena involving change.
- ☐ Be able to represent patterns and relationships in tables and graphs.
- ☐ Generate a generalised expression for linear patterns in words and algebraic expressions and fluently convert between each representation.
- ☐ Categorise patterns as linear or non-linear, using their defining characteristics as they appear in the different representations.

Sets

- ☐ Understand the concept of a set as a well-defined collection of elements.
- ☐ Understand that set equality is a relationship where two sets have the same elements.
- ☐ Define sets by listing their elements, if finite (including in a 2-set Venn diagram), or by generating rules that define them.
- ☐ Use and understand suitable set notation and terminology, including null set, $\varnothing$, subset, complement, element, $\in$, universal set, cardinal number, #, intersection, $\cap$, union, $\cup$, set difference, $\backslash$, $\mathbb{N}$, $\mathbb{Z}$, $\mathbb{Q}$, $\mathbb{R}$, and $\mathbb{R}\backslash\mathbb{Q}$.
- ☐ Perform the following operations on 2 sets
  - ○ intersection
  - ○ union (for three sets)
  - ○ set difference
  - ○ complement
- ☐ Be able to use brackets with set notation, to define the order of operations.

Functions

- [ ] Demonstrate understanding of the concept of a function.
- [ ] Represent and interpret functions in different ways:
  - graphically (for $x \in \mathbb{N}, \mathbb{Z}$, and $\mathbb{R}$, [continuous functions only], as appropriate)
  - diagrammatically
  - in words
  - algebraically
  - use the language and notation of functions (domain, range, co-domain, $f(x) = ,f:x \longmapsto$, and $y =$)
- [ ] Use graphical methods to find and interpret approximate solutions of equations such as $f(x) = g(x)$.
- [ ] Make connections between the shape of a graph and the story of a phenomenon, including identifying and interpreting maximum and minimum points.

Applied measure

- [ ] Calculate, interpret and apply units of measure and time.
- [ ] Solve problems that involve calculating average speed, distance and time.

Applied arithmetic

- [ ] Making value for money calculations and judgments.
- [ ] Use and understand ratio and proportion.
- [ ] Solve money-related problems that involve:
  - bills
  - currency conversion
  - VAT
  - profit or loss
  - percentage profit or loss
  - cost price
  - selling price
  - compound interest
  - income tax
  - net pay (including other deductions)
- [ ] Investigate situations involving proportionality so you can use absolute and relative comparison where appropriate.
- [ ] Solve problems involving proportionality including those involving:
  - currency conversion
  - average speed, distance, and time

1 # Number Systems

aims

☐ To learn what the symbols ℕ, ℤ, ℚ, and ℝ represent
☐ To be familiar with prime numbers, factors and the fundamental theorem of arithmetic
☐ To be able to find LCM and HCF as required

Natural numbers ℕ

The positive whole numbers 1, 2, 3, 4, 5, 6, . . . are also called the counting numbers. The dots indicate that the numbers go on forever and have no end (infinite).

exam
Q

Give two reasons why $-7 \cdot 3$ is not a natural number.

Solution

Reason 1. It is a negative number

Reason 2. It is not a whole number (it is a decimal)

Factors (divisors)

key
point

The factors of any whole number are the whole numbers that divide exactly into the given number, leaving no remainder.

1 is a factor of every number.

Every number is a factor of itself.

Example

Find the highest common factor of 18 and 45.

Solution

18		45	
1 × 18		1 × 45	
2 × 9		3 × 15	
3 × 6		5 × 9	

The common factors are 1, 3 and 9.

The highest common factor of 18 and 45 is 9.

key point

The highest common factor of two or more numbers is the largest factor that is common to each of the given numbers.

Example

In these productogons, the number in each square is the product of the numbers in the circles on each side of it. Find the missing numbers in each of these productogons.

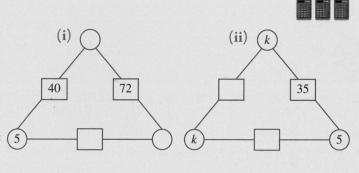

(i)

40   72

5   ☐   ○

(ii) k

☐   35

k ☐   5

Solution

key point

The use of the word productogon in the question indicates we use multiplication. This is because product means multiply.

(i)

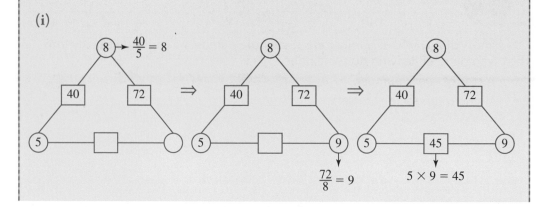

8 → $\frac{40}{5}$ = 8

40   72

5   ☐   ○

⟹

8

40   72

5   ☐   9

$\frac{72}{8}$ = 9

⟹

8

40   72

5   45   9

5 × 9 = 45

(ii)

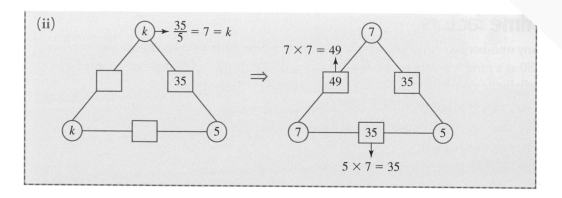

Prime numbers

A prime number is a whole number greater than 1 that has only two factors, 1 and itself.

The first 12 prime numbers are

2, 3, 5, 7, 11, 13, 17, 19, 23, 29, 31 and 37.

There is an infinite number of prime numbers.

Numbers that have more than two factors are called composite numbers, e.g. 20 has 1, 2, 4, 5, 10, 20 as factors.

The fundamental theorem of arithmetic states that any whole number greater than 1 can be written as the product of its prime factors in a **unique** way. This will underpin many exam questions on number theory.

ctors

can be expressed as a product of prime numbers. To express the number
luct of its prime numbers, first divide by the smallest prime number that
will divide exactly into it.

The smallest prime number 2 : $\quad 2 \mid 180$
The smallest prime 2 again   : $\quad 2 \mid 90$
The smallest prime 3   : $\quad 3 \mid 45$
The smallest prime 3 again   : $\quad 3 \mid 15$
The smallest prime 5   : $\quad 5 \mid 5$
$$\overline{1}$$

So 180 expressed as a product of primes is:

$$2 \times 2 \times 3 \times 3 \times 5 = 2^2 \times 3^2 \times 5$$

Example 1

For security, a credit card is encrypted using prime factors. A huge number is
assigned to each individual card and it can only be verified by its prime factor
decomposition. Find the 10-digit natural number which is assigned to the following
credit cards whose prime factor decomposition is

  (i) $2^2 \times 11 \times 13 \times 17^2 \times 19^3$

  (ii) $2^7 \times 3^2 \times 5^2 \times 7^3 \times 23 \times 31$

Solution

By calculator: (i)   1133847572

                 (ii) 7043299200

Example 2

Gepetto makes wooden puppets. He has three lengths of wood which
he wants to cut into pieces, all of which must be the same length and be as long as
possible. The lengths of the three pieces of wood are 315 cm, 357 cm and 252 cm.

  (i) Express each of the three lengths as a product of primes.

 (ii) Hence, calculate what length each piece should be and how many pieces he will
     have.

Solution

(i)

$$
\begin{array}{r|r}
3 & 315 \\
3 & 105 \\
5 & 35 \\
7 & 7 \\
& 1
\end{array}
$$

$$
\begin{array}{r|r}
3 & 357 \\
7 & 119 \\
17 & 17 \\
& 1
\end{array}
$$

$$
\begin{array}{r|r}
2 & 252 \\
2 & 126 \\
3 & 63 \\
3 & 21 \\
7 & 7 \\
& 1
\end{array}
$$

$3^2 \times 5 \times 7$ 　　　 $3 \times 7 \times 17$ 　　　 $2^2 \times 3^2 \times 7$

(ii) By observation of the three product of primes above, the highest common factor (HCF) is given by $3 \times 7 = 21$.

Hence, each piece of wood should be 21 cm long.

The number of pieces is given

by $\dfrac{315}{21} + \dfrac{357}{21} + \dfrac{252}{21}$

$= 15 + 17 + 12$

$= 44$

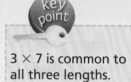

key point

3×7 is common to all three lengths.

Multiples and the lowest common multiple (LCM)

The multiples of a number are found by multiplying the number by 1, 2, 3 . . . and so on.

The multiples of 4 are: 4, 8, 12, 16, 20, . . .

The multiples of 7 are: 7, 14, 21, 28, 35, . . .

The **lowest common multiple** of two or more numbers is the **smallest multiple** that is common to each of the numbers.

In other words, the lowest common multiple is the **smallest** number into which each of the numbers will divide exactly.

For example, the lowest common multiple of 2, 4 and 7 is 28, as 28 is the smallest number into which 2, 4 and 7 will all divide exactly.

The lowest common multiple of two or more numbers is found with the following steps:

1. Write down the multiples of each number.
2. The lowest common multiple is the smallest (first) multiple they have in common.

Example

K is the set of natural numbers from 1 to 25, inclusive.

(i) List the elements of K that are multiples of 3.

(ii) List the elements of K that are multiples of 5.

(iii) Write down the lowest common multiple of 3 and 5.

Solution

$K = \{1, 2, 3, 4, 5, 6, 7, 8, 9, 10, 11, 12, 13, 14, 15, 16, 17, 18, 19, 20, 21, 22, 23, 24, 25\}$

(i) Multiples of $3 = \{3, 6, 9, 12, 15, 18, 21, 24\}$

(ii) Multiples of $5 = \{5, 10, 15, 20, 25\}$

(iii) Lowest common multiple (LCM) is 15.

That is the smallest number that both sets have in common.

Integers $\mathbb{Z}$

Negative numbers are numbers below zero. Positive and negative **whole** numbers, including zero, are called integers.

Integers can be represented on a number line:

Integers to the right of zero are called **positive integers**.

Integers to the left of zero are called **negative integers**.

Example

At midnight on Christmas Eve the temperatures in some cities were as shown in the table.

(i) Which city recorded the
   (a) Lowest temperature
   (b) Highest temperature?
(ii) List the temperatures from coldest to hottest.
(iii) Which cities had a temperature difference of 6°C?
(iv) What is the difference in temperature between
   (a) Dublin and Moscow
   (b) Cairo and Dublin?

New York	2°C
Rome	−2°C
Dublin	−1°C
Moscow	−20°C
Cairo	4°C

Solution

(i) (a) Lowest temperature, $-20°$, in Moscow.
   (b) Highest temperature, $4°$, in Cairo.
(ii) $-20, -2, -1, 2, 4$
(iii)

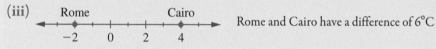

Rome and Cairo have a difference of 6°C

(iv) (a) Dublin and Moscow $= -1 - (-20) = -1 + 20 = 19°$
   (b) Cairo and Dublin $= 4 - (-1) = 4 + 1 = 5°$

Fractions (rational numbers)

A fraction is written as two whole numbers, one over the other, separated by a bar.
Equivalent fractions are fractions that are equal.
For example:

$$\frac{1}{3} = \frac{2}{6} = \frac{3}{9} = \frac{4}{12}$$

This can be shown on a diagram where the same proportion is shaded in each circle.

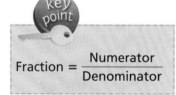

key point

$$\text{Fraction} = \frac{\text{Numerator}}{\text{Denominator}}$$

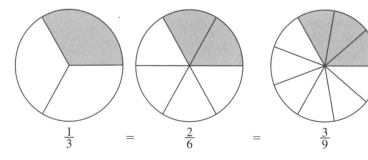

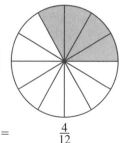

$$\frac{1}{3} = \frac{2}{6} = \frac{3}{9} = \frac{4}{12}$$

A rational number (fraction) is a number that can be written as a ratio, $\frac{p}{q}$, of two integers, p and q, but $q \neq 0$.

Examples are $\frac{7}{2}$, $-\frac{11}{19}$, $8 = \frac{8}{1}$, $0 = \frac{0}{1}$, $5 \cdot 23 = \frac{523}{100}$

Rational numbers are denoted by the letter $\mathbb{Q}$.

Example

Bren is trying to subtract $\frac{1}{5}$ from $\frac{7}{8}$.

His attempt is shown here: $\frac{7}{8} - \frac{1}{5} = \frac{6}{3} = 2.$

(i) Explain what Bren has done wrong.

(ii) Write out the correct solution.

Solution

(i) It seems that Bren has subtracted the top numbers and subtracted the bottom numbers.

For subtraction or addition of fractions, we must find a common denominator.

(ii) $\frac{7}{8} - \frac{1}{5} \Rightarrow$ common denominator $= 8 \times 5 = 40$

Then $\dfrac{7}{8} - \dfrac{1}{5} = \dfrac{(5)(7) - (8)(1)}{40} = \dfrac{35 - 8}{40} = \dfrac{27}{40}.$

See the chapter on algebraic expressions for more on addition/subtraction of fractions.

Sheila orders two pizzas to divide evenly between herself and five friends.

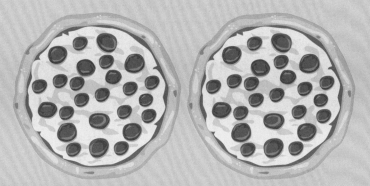

(i) What fraction of a pizza will each person get? Write your fraction in its simplest form.

(ii) One of the friends gets a text and leaves before the pizza is delivered. What fraction will each person now get if the pizzas are divided evenly between those remaining?

(iii) Find how much extra pizza each person gets.

Solution

(i) 2 pizzas ÷ 6 = $\dfrac{2}{6}$ = $\dfrac{1}{3}$ each

(ii) 2 pizzas ÷ 5 = $\dfrac{2}{5}$ each

(iii) Extra pizza = $\dfrac{2}{5} - \dfrac{1}{3}$

$= \dfrac{(2)(3) - (1)(5)}{15}$ (common denominator = 5 × 3 = 15)

$= \dfrac{6 - 5}{15}$

$= \dfrac{1}{15}$

Three students completed a test but got their results in different ways. The teacher told Karen that she got 0·7 of the questions correct. John was told he got 80% of the questions correct. David was told he got $\frac{3}{4}$ of the questions correct.

(i) Which student got the best result? Give a reason for your answer.

(ii) There were 20 questions on the test. How many questions each did Karen, John and David answer correctly?

(iii) Find the mean number of correct answers.

Solution

(i) Karen got $0·7 = \frac{7}{10} = \frac{7 \times 100}{10}\% = 70\%$

John got 80%

David got $\frac{3}{4} = \frac{3 \times 100}{4}\% = 75\%$

> **key point**
>
> Mean is covered in Statistics, in Book 2.

By observation from the above work, John got the best result.

(ii) Karen got 70% of $20 = \frac{70}{100} \times 20 = 14$ correct

John got 80% of $20 = \frac{80}{100} \times 20 = 16$ correct

David got 75% of $20 = \frac{75}{100} \times 20 = 15$ correct

(iii) Mean $= \frac{14 + 16 + 15}{3} = \frac{45}{3} = 15$

The question was awarded 20 marks in total, as follows.

Part **i** 10 marks, with 5 marks awarded for one correct piece of work.

Part **ii** 5 marks, with 3 marks awarded for one correct piece of work.

Part **iii** 5 marks, with 3 marks awarded for one correct piece of work.

Hence, with 11 marks out of 20 marks awarded for no correct answers, you can see the importance of attempting every part of every question.

exam Q

(a) Find the value of each of the following
    (i) 372 + 119   (ii) 3·4 × 7   (iii) 3 × (7 − 5)

(b) Shade in $\dfrac{3}{4}$ of the area of each shape. The shapes are labelled A and B.

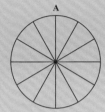

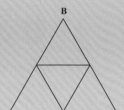

(c) Write the numbers **3, 9,** and **25** into the three empty boxes to make the mathematical statement true. Use each number only once.

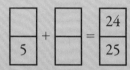

Solution

(a) You can use a calculator to find the value of each part:
    (i) 372 + 119   (ii) 3·4 × 7   (iii) 3 × (7 − 5)
      = 491   = 23·8   = 3 × 2   (simplify inside brackets first)
                                                  = 6

(b) Shape A is divided into 12 equal parts.

$$\frac{3}{4} \text{ of } 12 = 9$$

So, we need to shade in 9 of the 12 sectors:

Shape B is divided into 4 equal parts.

$$\frac{3}{4} \text{ of } 4 = 3$$

So, we need to shade in 3 of the 4 triangles:

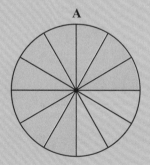

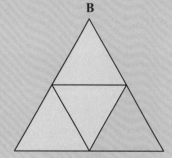

(c) Since the final result has a denominator of 25, the original denominators must both be factors of 25.

So, we can conclude that 25 goes into the position of the missing denominator.

Since the final result of $\dfrac{24}{25}$ is less than 1, in each case, the numerator must be less than the denominators. So, 3 goes above the 5 and 9 goes above the 25.

key point

You can use your calculator to verify the answer

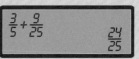

exam Q

(i) Write $\dfrac{3}{8}$ as a decimal.

(ii) Represent the numbers $\frac{3}{8}$ and 0·4 on the number line below.

(iii) How could the number line in (ii) above help you decide which is the bigger of the two numbers?

Solution

(i) $\dfrac{3}{8} = 0{·}375$

(ii)

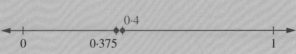

(iii) The number to the right-hand side on a number line is always the bigger of the two numbers.

0·4 is the bigger number.

Real numbers

The natural numbers ($\mathbb{N}$) are a subset of the integers ($\mathbb{Z}$).

The integers ($\mathbb{Z}$) are a subset of the rational numbers ($\mathbb{Q}$).

The rational numbers ($\mathbb{Q}$) are a subset of the real numbers ($\mathbb{R}$).

The number sets are in the formulae and tables booklet, which is available to you in the examination.

The following Venn diagram summarises the number system.

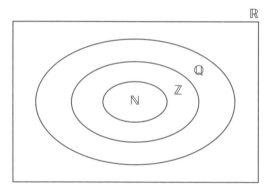

See the chapter on sets, where the first exam question illustrates the way the examiner links sets and the number system.

The numbers outside the set $\mathbb{Q}$ are called irrational numbers. You will study irrational numbers at Leaving Certificate.

The columns in the table below represent the following sets of numbers: natural numbers ($\mathbb{N}$), integers ($\mathbb{Z}$), rational numbers ($\mathbb{Q}$). Complete the table by writing either YES or NO into each box, indicating whether each of the numbers -23, $\frac{1}{2}$, 7^2, $2\cdot95$, 0, 47 is or is not an element of each.

(One box has already been filled in. The YES indicates that the number 47 is an element of the set of rational numbers, $\mathbb{Q}$.)

Set \ Number	-23	$\frac{1}{2}$	7^2	$2\cdot95$	0	47
$\mathbb{N}$						
$\mathbb{Z}$						
$\mathbb{Q}$						Yes

Solution

$7^2 = 49$ and 47 are the only natural numbers, $\mathbb{N}$, in the question. 49, 47, 0 and -23 are the only integers, $\mathbb{Z}$, and all six numbers are rational, $\mathbb{Q}$.

Set \ Number	-23	$\frac{1}{2}$	7^2	$2\cdot95$	0	47
$\mathbb{N}$	No	No	Yes	No	No	Yes
$\mathbb{Z}$	Yes	No	Yes	No	Yes	Yes
$\mathbb{Q}$	Yes	Yes	Yes	Yes	Yes	Yes

2 Algebraic Expressions

☐ To learn how to evaluate expressions
☐ To learn how to simplify algebraic expressions
☐ To learn how to add and subtract algebraic fractions

Evaluating expressions

To evaluate expressions given the value of the variables, substitute the values in for the variables and evaluate the expression. When replacing a letter with a number, it is **good practice to put the number in a bracket**.

Example

Find the value of $4x + 5$ when $x = 3$.

Solution

$4x + 5$
$4(3) + 5$ (let $x = 3$)
$12 + 5$
17

key point

Once you have substituted in the given values, you can use your calculator to simplify the calculations required.

Example

Find the value of $2a^2 - 11$ when $a = 4$.

Solution

$2a^2 - 11$
$2(4)^2 - 11$ (let $a = 4$)
$2(16) - 11$
$32 - 11$
21

exam focus

Evaluating expressions is a vital skill for you to have throughout all aspects of your maths course.

Example

If $p = -4$, find the value of:

(i) $3p + 5$

(ii) $2p^2 - 5$

key point

Take care when substituting in negative values. Always put brackets around these, then simplify the expression.

Solution

(i) $3p + 5$

  $3(-4) + 5$

  $-12 + 5$

  -7

(ii) $2p^2 - 5$

  $2(-4)^2 - 5$

  $2(16) - 5$

  $32 - 5$

  27

exam Q

Given that $y = \sqrt{2x - a}$,

find the value of y when $x = 4$ and $a = -1$.

Solution

$y = \sqrt{2x - a}$

$y = \sqrt{2(4) - (-1)}$

$y = \sqrt{8 + 1}$

$y = \sqrt{9}$

$y = 3$

exam Q

Find the values of the following expressions if $x = 3$ and $y = 5$.

(i) $5x + 4y$

(ii) $x^2 + y^2$

Solution

(i) $5x + 4y$ (let $x = 3$ and $y = 5$)

  $5(3) + 4(5)$

  $15 + 20$

  35

(ii) $x^2 + y^2$ (let $x = 3$ and $y = 5$)

  $(3)^2 + (5)^2$

  $9 + 25$

  34

Find the values of the following expressions if $a = 4$ and $b = -1$.

(i) $2a + 3b - 2$

(ii) $a^2 + b^2 + 4$

(iii) $\dfrac{a + 2b}{2}$

Solution

$a = 4$ and $b = -1$ in each case:

(i) $2a + 3b - 2$

$2(4) + 3(-1) - 2$

$8 - 3 - 2$

3

(ii) $a^2 + b^2 + 4$

$(4)^2 + (-1)^2 + 4$

$16 + 1 + 4$

21

(iii) $\dfrac{a + 2b}{2}$

$\dfrac{4 + 2(-1)}{2}$

$\dfrac{4 - 2}{2}$

$\dfrac{2}{2}$

1

Simplifying algebraic expressions

You must be able to apply the associative and distributive properties when simplifying algebraic expressions.

Associative property	Distributive property
$(A \times B) \times C = A \times (B \times C)$	$A(B + C) = AB + AC$
	$(A + B)(C + D) = A(C + D) + B(C + D)$

Example

Simplify $5(4x - 2) - 7(2x - 5)$.

Solution

$5(4x - 2) - 7(2x - 5)$ (remember, $-7 \times -5 = 35$)

$20x - 10 - 14x + 35$ (multiply out the brackets)

$6x + 25$ (add like terms)

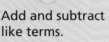

key point

Add and subtract like terms.

Example
Write in its simplest form: $(3x + 2y) - 2(x + 3y - 4)$.

Solution
$(3x + 2y) - 2(x + 3y - 4)$

$3x + 2y - 2x - 6y + 8$

$x - 4y + 8$

Example

Simplify $2a(4a + 3) - 4(3a - 7)$.

Solution
$2a(4a + 3) - 4(3a - 7)$

$8a^2 + 6a - 12a + 28$ (multiply out the brackets)

$8a^2 - 6a + 28$ (add like terms)

(i) Multiply $5(3a - 4b)$.

(ii) Multiply $x(x - y) + y(x + y)$. Write the answer in its simplest form.

Solution

(i) $5(3a - 4b)$

   $15a - 20b$

(ii) $x(x - y) + y(x + y)$

      $x^2 - xy + xy + y^2$

      $x^2 + y^2$

The entire question was worth 5 marks.

4 marks were awarded for getting either **(i)** or **(ii)** correct.

3 marks were awarded having any correct multiplication.

Example

Simplify $(x + 3)(x - 4)$.

Solution

Method 1: Use the distributive law

$(x + 3)(x - 4)$

$x(x - 4) + 3(x - 4)$ (remember, $+3 \times -4 = -12$)

$x^2 - 4x + 3x - 12$ (multiply out the brackets)

$x^2 - x - 12$ (add like terms)

Method 2: Use the box method

Put the terms in the first bracket on the top and terms from the second bracket down the side. Multiply each term by each other term.

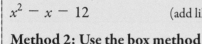

	x	$+3$
x	x^2	$+3x$
-4	$-4x$	-12

Listing all terms from inside the boxes:

$x^2 - 4x + 3x - 12$

$x^2 - x - 12$ (add like terms)

key point

There are two methods for multiplying out brackets. These are both shown in this example. You can use whichever method you prefer.

---

exam Q

Multiply $(3x - 2)$ by $(4x + 5)$ and write your answer in its simplest form.

Solution

Using the box method:

	$3x$	-2
$4x$	$12x^2$	$-8x$
5	$15x$	-10

$= 12x^2 + 15x - 8x - 10$

$= 12x^2 + 7x - 10$

key point

You can use either the distributive law **or** the box method to multiply out expressions. Use whichever method you are most comfortable with.

Example

Simplify $(3p + 2q)(p - 3q)$.

Solution

$(3p + 2q)(p - 3q)$

$3p(p - 3q) + 2q(p - 3q)$ (using the distributive law)

$3p^2 - 9pq + 2pq - 6q^2$ (multiply out the brackets)

$3p^2 - 7pq - 6q^2$ (add like terms)

Example

Simplify $(5a - 7)^2$.

Solution

$(5a - 7)^2 = (5a - 7)(5a - 7)$

key point

A common mistake here is for candidates to just square the first term and square the second term, getting $25a^2 + 49$. This is incorrect. You **must** multiply out as shown.

	$5a$	-7
$5a$	$25a^2$	$-35a$
-7	$-35a$	$+49$

$25a^2 - 35a - 35a + 49$ (using the box method)

$25a^2 - 70a + 49$ (add like terms)

exam Q

Multiply $(x - 2)$ by $(3x + 11)$ and hence evaluate your answer when $x = -2$.

Solution

Using the distributive law:

$(x - 2)(3x + 11)$

$x(3x + 11) - 2(3x + 11)$

$3x^2 + 11x - 6x - 22$ (multiply out the brackets)

$3x^2 + 5x - 22$ (add like terms)

exam focus

The word 'hence' means that you **must** simplify the expression first and **then** let $x = -2$.

Evaluate $3x^2 + 5x - 22$ when $x = -2$: $3(-2)^2 + 5(-2) - 22$

$3(4) - 10 - 22$

$12 - 32$

-20

Adding and subtracting algebraic fractions

Algebraic fractions that have numbers as denominators can be added or subtracted in exactly the same way as in arithmetic, i.e. we express the fractions with the lowest common denominator (the LCM of the denominators). Adding fractions was covered in the chapter on number systems.

Algebraic fractions are added or subtracted with the following steps:

1. Put brackets in where necessary.
2. Find the LCM of the expressions on the bottom.
3. Proceed in exactly the same way as in arithmetic.
4. Simplify the top (add and subtract terms which are the same).

Study the next example to understand the steps involved in adding and subtracting algebraic fractions.

Example

Write as a simple fraction: $\dfrac{x}{3} + \dfrac{5x}{6}$.

Solution

$$\frac{x}{3} + \frac{5x}{6}$$

$$\frac{?(x) + ?(5x)}{6} \qquad \text{(the LCM of the denominators is 6)}$$

$$\frac{2(x) + ?(5x)}{6} \qquad \text{(3 divides into 6 two times.}$$
$$\qquad\qquad\qquad\quad \text{Multiply 2 by the term on top of the 3.)}$$

$$\frac{2(x) + 1(5x)}{6} \qquad \text{(6 divides into 6 one time.}$$
$$\qquad\qquad\qquad\quad \text{Multiply 1 by the term on top of the 6.)}$$

$$\frac{2x + 5x}{6} \qquad \text{(multiply out the brackets)}$$

$$\frac{7x}{6} \qquad \text{(simplify)}$$

Example

Express $\dfrac{x+7}{3} - \dfrac{x}{9}$ as a single fraction.

Give your answer in its simplest form.

Solution

$\dfrac{(x+7)}{3} - \dfrac{(x)}{9}$ (put brackets on top)

$\dfrac{?(x+7) - ?(x)}{9}$ (LCM of the denominators 3 and 9 is 9)

$\dfrac{3(x+7) - ?(x)}{9}$ (3 divides into 9 three times.

Multiply 3 by the term on top of the 3.)

$\dfrac{3(x+7) - 1(x)}{9}$ (9 divides into 9 one time.

Multiply 1 by the term on top of the 9.)

$\dfrac{3x + 21 - x}{9}$ (multiply out the brackets)

$\dfrac{2x + 21}{9}$ (simplify the top)

Express $\dfrac{x+3}{2} + \dfrac{2x-1}{5}$ as a single fraction.

Solution

$\dfrac{(x+3)}{2} + \dfrac{(2x-1)}{5}$ (put brackets on top)

$\dfrac{?(x+3) + ?(2x-1)}{10}$ (LCM of the denominators 2 and 5 is 10)

$\dfrac{5(x+3) + ?(2x-1)}{10}$ (2 divides into 10 five times.

Multiply 5 by the term on top of the 2.)

$\dfrac{5(x+3) + 2(2x-1)}{10}$ (5 divides into 10 two times.

Multiply 2 by the term on top of the 5.)

$\dfrac{5x + 15 + 4x - 2}{10}$ (multiply out the brackets)

$\dfrac{9x + 13}{10}$ (simplify the top)

3 Factorising

Factorising and simplifying expressions

There are four types of factorising that we will meet on this course:

Take out the common terms	Factorising by grouping
$ab + ad = a(b + d)$	$ab + ad + cb + cd = (a + c)(b + d)$
Factorise a trinomial (three terms)	**Difference of two squares**
$a^2 - 2ab + b^2 = (a - b)(a - b)$	$a^2 - b^2 = (a + b)(a - b)$

Factorising is the reverse process of expanding brackets. You could use the box method to verify your factors.

	a	b
a	a^2	ab
$-b$	$-ab$	$-b^2$

$$= a^2 - ab + ab - b^2$$
$$= a^2 - b^2$$

1. Take out common terms

1. Find the highest common factor (HCF) of all the terms making up the expression. This is the biggest value (constants of variables) which divides into all terms evenly.
2. Put the HCF outside the brackets.
3. Divide each term by the HCF to find the factor inside the brackets.

Example

Factorise the following:

(i) $4x + 8$ (ii) $12ab + 9a$

Solution

(i) $4x + 8$ (HCF is 4)

$4(? + ?)$ (take out the 4)

$4(x + 2)$

(ii) $12ab + 9a$ (HCF is $3a$)

$3a(? + ?)$ (take out the $3a$)

$3a(4b + 3)$

Example

Factorise the following:

(i) $3p^2 + 6pq + 9p$ (ii) $2a^2b + 3ab^2$

Solution

(i) $3p^2 + 6pq + 9p$

$3pp + 6pq + 9p$ (HCF is $3p$)

$3p(p + 2q + 3)$ (factorise out $3p$)

(ii) $2a^2b + 3ab^2$

$2aab + 3abb$ (HCF is ab)

$ab(2a + 3b)$ (factorise out ab)

Factorise the following:

(i) $20xy - 4x^2$ (ii) $18a^3 + 24ab$

Solution

(i) $20xy - 4x^2$

$20xy - 4xx$ (HCF is $4x$)

$4x(5y - x)$ (factorise out $4x$)

(ii) $18a^3 + 24ab$

$18aaa + 24ab$ (HCF is $6a$)

$6a(3a^2 + 4b)$ (factorise out $6a$)

2. Factorising by grouping

Use this method when you have four terms with no common factor.

1. Group into pairs with a common factor.
2. Take out the HCF in each pair separately.
3. Take out the new common factor.

Example

Factorise the following:

(i) $3a - 3b + ac - bc$

(ii) $3pr - 3ps + qr - qs$

Solution

(i) $3a - 3b + ac - bc$ (already in pairs with a common factor)

$3(a - b) + c(a - b)$ (take out the common factor, in each pair)

$(a - b)(3 + c)$ (take out the common factor $(a - b)$)

(ii) $3pr - 3ps + qr - qs$ (already in pairs with a common factor)

$3p(r - s) + q(r - s)$ (take out the common factor, in each pair)

$(r - s)(3p + q)$ (take out the common factor $(r - s)$)

Example

Factorise the following:

(i) $7b - cb + 7c - c^2$

(ii) $6p - 2c + 3pc - c^2$

Solution

(i) $7b - cb + 7c - c^2$ (already in pairs with a common factor)

$b(7 - c) + c(7 - c)$ (take out the common factor in each pair)

$(7 - c)(b + c)$ (take out the common factor $(7 - c)$)

(ii) $6p - 2c + 3pc - c^2$ (already in pairs with a common factor)

$2(3p - c) + c(3p - c)$ (take out the common factor in each pair)

$(3p - c)(2 + c)$ (take out the common factor $(3p - c)$)

Factorise the following:

(i) $3xy - 10x - 10b + 3by$ **(ii)** $4c^2 - 3d - 2cd + 6c$

Solution

(i) $3xy - 10x - 10b + 3by$	(already in pairs with a common factor)
$x(3y - 10) + b(-10 + 3y)$	(take out the common factor in each pair)
$x(3y - 10) + b(3y - 10)$	(reorder the second bracket)
$(3y - 10)(x + b)$	(take out the common factor $(3y - 10)$)
(ii) $4c^2 - 3d - 2cd + 6c$	(no common factors in the first pair. Need to rearrange.)
$4c^2 - 2cd + 6c - 3d$	(rearrange order of the terms so that they are grouped into pairs with a common factor)
$2c(2c - d) + 3(2c - d)$	(take out the common factor in each pair)
$(2c - d)(2c + 3)$	(take out the common factor $(2c - d)$)

The sign is part of the term directly after it. Take care when rearranging the terms. Keep the sign with each term.

3. Quadratic trinomials

An expression in the form $x^2 + bx + c$, where b and c are numbers, is called a quadratic trinomial. This is because in the expression, the highest power of x is 2 (quadratic) and it contains three terms (trinomial).

For factorising, quadratic trinomials can be broken into two types:

1. **Final term is positive**

   When the final term is positive, the signs inside the middle of the brackets will be the **same**, either two pluses or two minuses. Keep the sign of the middle term given in the question.

2. **Final term is negative**

   When the final term is negative, the signs inside the middle of the brackets will be **different**. (i.e. one positive and one negative).

Some quadratic trinomials can be very challenging to factorise. Do not be discouraged! If you cannot find the correct factors straight away, keep going until you have tried all options.

Example

Factorise $x^2 + 8x + 15$.

Solution

$x^2 + 8x + 15$ (final term, $+15$, is positive, so the signs in the brackets are the same)

$(x + 3)(x + 5)$

Check: outside terms $= (x)(5) = 5x$

         inside terms $= (3)(x) = \underline{3x}$

            sum $=$ $8x =$ middle term of original quadratic trinomial

Therefore, factors $(x + 3)(x + 5)$ are correct.

key point

Use trial and improvement to find the factors. Multiply the inside terms, multiply the outside terms and add the results to see if you get the middle term of the original quadratic trinomial.

Check your answers:

	x	3
x	x^2	$3x$
5	$5x$	15

$= x^2 + 5x + 3x + 15$

$= x^2 + 8x + 15$

Alternative method:

$1x^2 + 8x + 15$ $1 \times 15 = 15$ (15 is the guide number: it tells you that

M   A   M   both signs are the same)

We need factors of 15 which add to give 8.

M = 15	A = 8
$1 \times 15 = 15$	$1 + 15 = 16$
$3 \times 5 = 15$	$3 + 5 = 8$

Check these values on a calculator if you are not confident with integers.

The factors which fit this criteria are 3 and 5.

Rewrite the trinomial, replacing $8x$ with $3x$ and $5x$.

$1x^2 + 3x + 5x + 15$

$x(x + 3) + 5(x + 3)$ (factorise by grouping)

$(x + 3)(x + 5)$

Example

Factorise $x^2 - 7x + 10$.

Solution

$x^2 - 7x + 10$ (final term, $+10$, is positive, so the signs in the brackets are the same)

$(x - 2)(x - 5)$

Check: outside terms $= (x)(-5) = -5x$

          inside terms $= (-2)(x) = \underline{-2x}$

                sum $=$ $-7x =$ middle term of original quadratic trinomial

Therefore, factors $(x - 2)(x - 5)$ are correct.

Check your answers:

	x	-2
x	x^2	$-2x$
-5	$-5x$	10

$= x^2 - 2x - 5x + 10$

$= x^2 - 7x + 10$

Alternative method:

$1x^2 - 7x + 10$ $1 \times 10 = 10$ (10 is the guide number: it tells you that

M   A   M   both signs are the same)

We need factors of 10 which add to give -7.

$M = 10$	$A = -7$
$1 \times 10 = 10$	$1 + 10 = 11$
$2 \times 5 = 10$	$2 + 5 = 7$
$-2 \times -5 = 10$	$-2 - 5 = -7$

The factors which fit this criteria are -2 and -5.

Rewrite the trinomial, replacing $-7x$ with $-2x$ and $-5x$.

$1x^2 - 2x - 5x + 10$

$x(x - 2) - 5(x - 2)$ (factorise by grouping)

$(x - 2)(x - 5)$

Example

Factorise $x^2 + 2x - 8$.

Solution

$x^2 + 2x - 8$ (final term, -8, is negative, so the signs in the brackets are different)

$(x + 4)(x - 2)$

Check: outside terms $= (x)(-2) = -2x$

inside terms $= (4)(x) \quad = \quad 4x$

sum $= \qquad\qquad 2x =$ middle term of original quadratic trinomial

Therefore, factors $(x + 4)(x - 2)$ are correct.

Check your answers:

	x	4
x	x^2	$4x$
-2	$-2x$	-8

$= x^2 + 4x - 2x - 8$

$= x^2 + 2x - 8$

Alternative method:

$1x^2 + 2x - 8 \qquad\qquad 1 \times -8 = -8$ (-8 is the guide number: it tells you that

M   A   M   the signs are different)

We need factors of -8 which add to give $+2$.

$M = -8$	$A = 2$
$1 \times -8 = -8$	$1 - 8 = -7$
$-1 \times 8 = -8$	$-1 + 8 = 7$
$-2 \times 4 = -8$	$-2 + 4 = 2$
$2 \times -4 = -8$	$2 - 4 = -2$

The factors which fit this criteria are 4 and -2.

Rewrite the trinomial, replacing $2x$ with $4x$ and $-2x$.

$1x^2 + 4x - 2x - 8$

$x(x + 4) - 2(x + 4)$ (factorise by grouping)

$(x + 4)(x - 2)$

Example

Factorise $x^2 - x - 12$.

Solution

$x^2 - x - 12$ (final term, -12, is negative, so the signs in the brackets are different)

$(x - 4)(x + 3)$

Check: outside terms $= (x)(3) = 3x$

           inside terms $= (-4)(x) = \underline{-4x}$

                 sum $= -x =$ middle term of original quadratic

                                         trinomial

Therefore, factors $(x - 4)(x + 3)$ are correct.

Check your answers:

	x	-4
x	x^2	$-4x$
3	$3x$	-12

$= x^2 - 4x + 3x - 12$

$= x^2 - x - 12$

Alternative method:

$1x^2 - x - 12$ $1 \times -12 = -12$ (-12 is the guide number: it tells you that
M   A   M   the signs are different)

We need factors of -12 which add to give -1.

$M = -12$	$A = -1$
$1 \times -12 = -12$	$1 - 12 = -11$
$-1 \times 12 = -12$	$-1 + 12 = 11$
$2 \times -6 = -12$	$2 - 6 = -4$
$-2 \times 6 = -12$	$-2 + 6 = 4$
$3 \times -4 = -12$	$3 - 4 = -1$
$-3 \times 4 = -12$	$-3 + 4 = 1$

The factors which fit this criteria are -4 and 3.

Rewrite the trinomial, replacing $-x$ with $-4x$ and $3x$.

$1x^2 - 4x + 3x - 12$

$x(x - 4) + 3(x - 4)$ (factorise by grouping)

$(x - 4)(x + 3)$

4. Difference of two squares

An expression such as $a^2 - b^2$ is called the difference of two squares.

1. Write each term as a perfect square with brackets.
2. Use the rule $a^2 - b^2 = (a - b)(a + b)$

key point

The difference of two squares is a special case of a trinomial. $x^2 - 25$ can be written as $x^2 + 0x - 25$ and factorised as $(x + 5)(x - 5)$.

Example

Factorise the following:

(i) $x^2 - 16$ (ii) $y^2 - 49$

Solution

(i) $x^2 - 16$
   $x^2 - (4)^2$
   $(x + 4)(x - 4)$

(ii) $y^2 - 49$
   $(y)^2 - (7)^2$
   $(y + 7)(y - 7)$

key point

Notice that the brackets are the same except for having opposite signs.

Example

Factorise the following:

(i) $p^2 - 64$

(ii) $3x^2 - 12$

Solution

(i) $p^2 - 64$

$(p)^2 - (8)^2$

$(p + 8)(p - 8)$

(ii) $3x^2 - 12$

$3(x^2 - 4)$ (take out the common factor)

$3(x^2 - (2)^2)$

$3(x + 2)(x - 2)$

Preparing for the exam

You must practise the previous four different types of factorising and be able to recognise when to use each type. In the exam you may be given a number of expressions to factorise. It is up to you to know which method of factorising to use.

The following steps should help you to determine which type of factorising to use:

1. Check for common factors — if there are any, factorise these out.
2. Are there four terms for factorising by grouping?
3. Is it a quadratic trinomial, in the form $x^2 + bx + c$?
4. Are there only two terms? Are they squares? If so, use the difference of two squares.

Example

Factorise fully each of the following:

(i) $20xy - 4x^2$

(ii) $ax + 2ay + 3x + 6y$

Solution

(i) Take out common factors:

$20xy - 4x^2$

$20xy - 4xx$ (HCF is $4x$)

$4x(5y - x)$

(ii) Factorise by grouping:

$ax + 2ay + 3x + 6y$

$a(x + 2y) + 3(x + 2y)$

$(x + 2y)(a + 3)$

exam Q

Factorise fully each of the following expressions:

(i) $5x^3 - 10x^2$

(ii) $x^2 - 81$

(iii) $a^2 - ab + 3a - 3b$

Solution

(i) To factorise $5x^3 - 10x^2$, you must take out common factors.

$5x^3 - 10x^2$

$5xxx - 10xx$ (HCF is $5xx$)

$5xx(x - 2)$ (factorise out $5xx$)

$5x^2(x - 2)$ ($5xx = 5x^2$)

(ii) To factorise $x^2 - 81$, you must find the difference of two squares.

$x^2 - 81$

$(x)^2 - (9)^2$

$(x + 9)(x - 9)$

(iii) To factorise $a^2 - ab + 3a - 3b$, you must factorise by grouping.

$a^2 - ab + 3a - 3b$

$aa - ab + 3a - 3b$

$a(a - b) + 3(a - b)$

$(a - b)(a + 3)$

exam focus

As shown here, you may be asked to use different types of factorising in the one exam question. You must be able to recognise which type of factorising is needed in each case.

exam Q

Factorise fully each of the following expressions:

(i) $4xy - 6x^2y^2$

(ii) $2ax - ay + 2bx - by$

Solution

(i) To factorise $4xy - 6x^2y^2$ you must take out common factors.

$4xy - 6x^2y^2$

$4xy - 6xxyy$ (HCF is $2xy$)

$2xy(2 - 3xy)$

(ii) To factorise $2ax - ay + 2bx - by$, you must factorise by grouping.

> This question was worth 10 marks, with 8 marks awarded for correctly factorising either part **(i) or (ii)**.

$2ax - ay + 2bx - by$

$a(2x - y) + b(2x - y)$ (take the common factors out of each pair)

$(2x - y)(a + b)$ (take out the common factor $(2x - y)$)

(i) There are four terms given below. Three of them have a common factor other than 1.

$$3xy \qquad\qquad 6ay \qquad\qquad 11ax \qquad\qquad 9y$$

Underline these three terms and write down the highest common factor of the three terms.

(ii) Factorise fully each of the following expressions:

   (a) $4x + 8y - 12z$ **(b)** $ab - 2a + 3b - 6$

   (c) $x^2 + 5x + 6$ **(d)** $b^2 - 16$

Solution

(i) The three terms which have a common factor other than 1 are underlined.

$$\underline{3xy} \qquad\qquad \underline{6ay} \qquad\qquad 11ax \qquad\qquad \underline{9y}$$

The highest common factor of these three terms is $3y$.

(ii) Factorise each of the following.

   (a) To factorise $4x + 8y - 12z$, you must take out any common factors.

      $4x + 8y - 12z$ (HCF is 4)

      $4(x + 2y - 3z)$

(b) To factorise $ab - 2a + 3b - 6$, you must factorise by grouping.

$ab - 2a + 3b - 6$

$a(b - 2) + 3(b - 2)$ (take the common factors out of each pair)

$(b - 2)(a + 3)$ (take out the common factors $(b - 2)$)

(c) To factorise $x^2 + 5x + 6$, you must factorise a quadratic trinomial.

We need factors of 6 which add up to 5. These factors are 2 and 3.

$(x + 2)(x + 3)$

(d) To factorise $b^2 - 16$, you must factorise the difference of two squares.

$b^2 - (4)^2$

$(b + 4)(b - 4)$

This question had five parts to answer. (Part **(i)** was taken as one part.)
The entire question was worth 10 marks.
8 marks were awarded for getting any three of the five parts correct.
7 marks were awarded for getting any one of the five parts correct.
5 marks were awarded for any correct attempt shown.
Make sure you attempt all questions. There are no marks for blanks!

(a) Factorise the quadratic expression $x^2 + 2x - 3$.

(b) Factorise fully $3ps - pr + 3qs - qr$.

Solution

(a) $x^2 + 2x - 3$ (need factors of -3 which add up to $+2$: -1 and $+3$)

$x^2 - 1x + 3x - 3$ (rewrite the $+2x$ term as $-1x + 3x$)

$x(x - 1) + 3(x - 1)$ (factorise out the common factors in each pair of terms)

$(x - 1)(x + 3)$ (factorise the common bracket $(x - 1)$ out of each part)

(b) $3ps - pr + 3qs - qr$ (already in pairs with a common factor)

$p(3s - r) + q(3s - r)$ (factorise out the common factors in each pair of terms)

$(3s - r)(p + q)$ (factorise the common bracket $(3s - r)$ out of each part)

(i) Factorise $4x^2 - 12x$.

(ii) Factorise $x^2 - 6x + 9$.

(iii) Simplify $\dfrac{4x^2 - 12x}{x^2 - 6x + 9}$.

Solution

(i) $4x^2 - 12x$ (HCF is $4x$)

    $4x(x - 3)$ (factorise out $4x$)

(ii) $x^2 - 6x + 9$

    $(x - 3)(x - 3)$

(iii) $\dfrac{4x^2 - 12x}{x^2 - 6x + 9}$

$\dfrac{4x(x - 3)}{(x - 3)(x - 3)}$

$\dfrac{4x}{x - 3}$

Simplify $\dfrac{x^2 + x - 20}{3x - 12}$.

Solution

$\dfrac{(x + 5)(x - 4)}{3(x - 4)}$ (factorise the top and bottom)

$\dfrac{x + 5}{3}$ (divide the top and bottom by $(x - 4)$)

Simplify $\dfrac{x^2 + 7x + 12}{x^2 + 2x - 3}$.

Solution

$\dfrac{(x + 3)(x + 4)}{(x + 3)(x - 1)}$ (factorise the top and bottom)

$\dfrac{x + 4}{x - 1}$ (divide the top and bottom by $(x + 3)$)

aims
☐ To learn how to solve linear equations
☐ To learn how to form and solve linear equations in in-context questions

An equation is solved with the following method:

Whatever you do to one side, you must do exactly the same to the other side.

Note: Keep balance in mind.
The solution of an equation is the number that makes both sides balance.

Example
Find the value of x given that $2x - 7 = 23$.

Solution
$$2x - 7 = 23$$
$$2x - 7 + 7 = 23 + 7 \quad \text{(add 7 to both sides)}$$
$$2x = 30 \quad \text{(simplify)}$$
$$x = 15 \quad \text{(divide both sides by 2)}$$

Solve $3(x - 2) + 1 = 19$.

Solution

$$3(x - 2) + 1 = 19$$
$$3x - 6 + 1 = 19 \quad \text{(multiply out the brackets)}$$
$$3x - 5 = 19 \quad \text{(simplify)}$$
$$3x - 5 + 5 = 19 + 5 \quad \text{(add 5 to both sides)}$$
$$3x = 24 \quad \text{(simplify)}$$
$$x = 8 \quad \text{(divide both sides by 3)}$$

Example

Solve the equation: $-2(x - 3) = 10$.

Solution

$$-2(x - 3) = 10$$
$$-2x + 6 = 10 \qquad \text{(multiply out)}$$
$$-2x + 6 - 6 = 10 - 6 \qquad \text{(subtract 6 from both sides)}$$
$$-2x = 4 \qquad \text{(simplify)}$$
$$x = -2 \qquad \text{(divide both sides by } -2)$$

Example

Solve the equation $3(x - 2) = 2x + 5$.

Solution

$$3(x - 2) = 2x + 5$$
$$3x - 6 = 2x + 5 \qquad \text{(remove brackets)}$$
$$3x - 6 + 6 = 2x + 5 + 6 \qquad \text{(add 6 to both sides)}$$
$$3x = 2x + 11 \qquad \text{(simplify)}$$
$$3x - 2x = 2x + 11 - 2x \qquad \text{(subtract } 2x \text{ from both sides)}$$
$$x = 11 \qquad \text{(simplify)}$$

exam Q

Solve the equation $3(2x - 7) = 5(x - 1)$.

Solution

$$3(2x - 7) = 5(x - 1)$$
$$6x - 21 = 5x - 5 \qquad \text{(remove brackets)}$$
$$6x - 21 - 5x = 5x - 5 - 5x \qquad \text{(subtract } 5x \text{ from both sides)}$$
$$x - 21 = -5 \qquad \text{(simplify)}$$
$$x - 21 + 21 = -5 + 21 \qquad \text{(add 21 to both sides)}$$
$$x = 16 \qquad \text{(add 21 to both sides)}$$

Solve the equation $5(3x + 1) - 2(5x + 35) = 0$.

Verify your answer.

Solution

$5(3x + 1) - 2(5x + 35) = 0$

$15x + 5 - 10x - 70 = 0$ (remove brackets)

$5x - 65 = 0$ (simplify)

$5x - 65 + 65 = 65$ (add 65 to both sides)

$5x = 65$ (simplify)

$x = \dfrac{65}{5}$ (divide both sides by 5)

$x = 13$

To verify your answer, let $x = 13$ in the original equation:

$5(3x + 1) - 2(5x + 35) = 0$

$5(3(13) + 1) - 2(5(13) + 35) = 0$

$5(39 + 1) - 2(65 + 35) = 0$

$5(40) - 2(100) = 0$

$200 - 200 = 0$

$0 = 0$

The equation is balanced, therefore we have verified our answer.

Real-life applications to solving equations

You will often be required to solve an equation which has been given in a real-world situation. These are also called in-context problems.

These real-life applications can appear in various topics throughout your course. Be aware that these questions may not always look like algebra.

Example

Zach drove from Town A to Town B, a distance of x km.

He then drove from Town B to Town C, a distance of $(2x + 1)$ km.

The total distance that he drove was 55 km. Find the value of x.

Hence, find the distance between Town A and Town B and also Town B and Town C.

Solution

Total distance = (Town A to Town B) + (Town B to Town C)

$$55 = (x) + (2x + 1)$$
$$55 = x + 2x + 1 \quad \text{(remove brackets)}$$
$$55 = 3x + 1 \quad \text{(simplify)}$$
$$55 - 1 = 3x + 1 - 1 \quad \text{(subtract 1 from both sides)}$$
$$54 = 3x \quad \text{(simplify)}$$
$$18 = x \quad \text{(divide both sides by 3)}$$

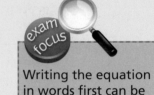

Writing the equation in words first can be helpful.

Town A to Town B = x m = 18 km

Town B to Town C = $2x + 1 = 2(18) + 1 = 36 + 1 = 37$ km

Example

Amy has €x. James has €6 more than Amy.

(i) How much money does James have, in terms of x?

(ii) If Amy and James have €16 in total, write an equation in x to show this information.

(iii) Solve the equation to find how much money Amy has.

Solution

(i) James has €6 more than Amy.

　　James has €$(6 + x)$.

(ii) Amy + James = 16

　　$x + (6 + x) = 16$

(iii) Solve:

'in terms of x' means that the variable x must be in your answer.

$$x + (6 + x) = 16$$
$$x + 6 + x = 16 \quad \text{(remove brackets)}$$
$$2x + 6 = 16 \quad \text{(simplify)}$$
$$2x + 6 - 6 = 16 - 6 \quad \text{(subtract 6 from both sides)}$$
$$2x = 10 \quad \text{(simplify)}$$
$$x = 5 \quad \text{(divide both sides by 2)}$$

Therefore, Amy has €5.

Example

(i) Eoin is t years of age.

Katie is 4 years older than Eoin.

Laura is twice as old as Eoin.

Write Katie's age and Laura's age in terms of t.

(ii) From part **(i)**, the sum of Eoin's age, Katie's age and Laura's age is 52.

Write down an equation in t to represent this information.

(iii) Solve your equation to find Eoin's age in years.

Solution

(i) Eoin is t years of age.

Katie is 4 years older than Eoin. Therefore, Katie is $(t + 4)$ years old.

Laura is twice as old as Eoin. Therefore, Laura is $(2t)$ years old.

(ii) (Eoin's age) + (Katie's age) + (Laura's age) = 52

$$(t) + (t + 4) + (2t) = 52$$

(iii) Solve $(t) + (t + 4) + (2t) = 52$

$t + t + 4 + 2t = 52$	(remove brackets)
$4t + 4 = 52$	(simplify)
$4t + 4 - 4 = 52 - 4$	(subtract 4 from both sides)
$4t = 48$	(simplify)
$t = 12$	(divide both sides by 4)

Therefore, Eoin is 12 years old.

(i) The cost of a DVD is €x. The cost of a CD is €3 less.

What is the cost of a CD in terms of x?

(ii) The total cost of three DVDs and two CDs is €54.

Write an equation in x to represent this information.

(iii) Solve your equation to find the cost of a DVD.

Solution

(i) DVD = €x

CD = cost of DVD − 3

CD = €$(x − 3)$

(ii) The total cost of three DVDs and two CDs is €54.

$$3(x) + 2(x - 3) = 54$$

(iii) Solve: $3(x) + 2(x - 3) = 54$

$3x + 2x - 6 = 54$	(remove brackets)
$5x - 6 = 54$	(simplify)
$5x - 6 + 6 = 54 + 6$	(add 6 to both sides)
$5x = 60$	(simplify)
$x = 12$	(divide both sides by 5)

Hence, a DVD costs €12

exam Q

(i) Conor spent €y on a book. He then spent €(4y + 6) on a football jersey. In total, he spent €61.

Write an equation in y to represent this information.

(ii) Solve your equation from **(i)** to find the value of y.

(iii) Hence, find the cost of the book and the cost of the football jersey that Conor bought.

Solution

(i) Book + Football jersey = €61

$$(y) + (4y + 6) = 61$$

(ii) Solve: $(y) + (4y + 6) = 61$

$y + 4y + 6 = 61$	(remove brackets)
$5y + 6 = 61$	
$5y = 61 - 6$	(subtract 6 from both sides)
$5y = 55$	
$y = \dfrac{55}{5}$	(divide both sides by 5)
$y = 11$	

(iii) Book: €y = €11

Jersey: €4y + 6 = €4(11) + 6 = €44 + 6 = €50

Clodagh tests the knowledge of her two younger sisters, Anna and Lauren.

(i) Clodagh says that the sum of two consecutive numbers is 35. Anna answers that the numbers are 20 and 15. Lauren says that the numbers are 17 and 18. Which sister is right? Give a reason for your answer.

(ii) Clodagh then says, 'When 8 is added to three times a number, the result is 47'.

Anna works out the correct answer, which is 13.

Show one method Anna could have used to get the correct answer.

key point

Consecutive means one after another.

Solution

(i) Anna is incorrect, as although the sum of the numbers 20 and 15 is 35, the numbers are not consecutive numbers.

Lauren is correct, as the sum of the numbers 17 and 18 is 35, and the numbers are consecutive numbers.

(ii) Let the number be x:

When 8 is added to three times a number, the result is 47.

$$8 + 3x = 47$$
$$8 + 3x - 8 = 47 - 8 \qquad \text{(subtract 8 from both sides)}$$
$$3x = 39 \qquad \text{(simplify)}$$
$$x = 13 \qquad \text{(divide both sides by 3)}$$

exam focus

Part **(i)** was worth 5 marks, with 3 marks awarded for partial credit, for example giving the correct answer with an incorrect reason, or an incorrect answer but the correct reason.

Part **(ii)** was worth 5 marks, with 3 marks awarded for partial credit.

Jane sets Molly a word problem. 'If I multiply a number by 7 and add 4, the result is the same as multiplying the number by 3 and taking away 8.' Molly starts by writing $7x + 4 =$.

Finish Molly's equation and solve it to find the number.

Solution

Letting the number be x:

Multiply a number by 7 and add 4. The result is the same as multiplying the number by 3 and taking away 8.

$$7x + 4 = 3x - 8$$

$7x + 4 - 3x = 3x - 8 - 3x$ (subtract $3x$ from both sides)

$4x + 4 = -8$ (simplify)

$4x + 4 - 4 = -8 - 4$ (subtract 4 from both sides)

$4x = -12$ (simplify)

$$\frac{4x}{4} = \frac{-12}{4}$$ (divide both sides by 4)

$$x = -3$$

This exam question was not well answered by candidates. Consequently, the entire question was worth 2 marks. One mark was awarded for correctly completing the equation and the second mark was awarded for solving the equation.

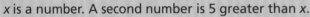

x is a number. A second number is 5 greater than x.

  (i) Write down the second number in terms of x.

  (ii) Twice the first number added to three times the second number is equal to 35. Write down an equation in x to represent this information.

 (iii) Solve your equation for x and state what the two numbers are.

 (iv) Verify your result.

Solution

  (i) A second number is 5 greater than x, therefore the second number is $x + 5$.

  (ii) Twice the first number added to three times the second number is equal to 35.

$$2(\text{first number}) + 3(\text{second number}) = 35$$
$$2(x) + 3(x + 5) = 35$$

(iii) Solve: $2(x) + 3(x + 5) = 35$

$2x + 3x + 15 = 35$	(remove brackets)
$5x + 15 = 35$	(simplify)
$5x + 15 - 15 = 35 - 15$	(subtract 15 from both sides)
$5x = 20$	(simplify)
$x = 4$	(divide both sides by 5)

First number $= x = 4$

Second number $= x + 5 = 4 + 5 = 9$

(iv) To verify the results, see if 2(first number) + 3(second number) = 35

$$2(\text{first number}) + 3(\text{second number})$$
$$2(4) + 3(9)$$
$$8 + 27$$
$$35$$

Therefore, we have verified our results.

The length of a rectangle is $(3x + 11)$ units and the width is $(5x - 23)$
units, as shown in the diagram.

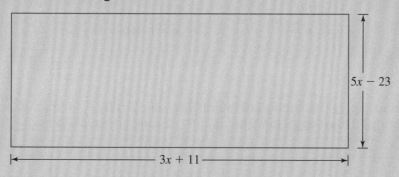

(i) Find, in terms of x, the perimeter of the rectangle.

(ii) If the perimeter is 88 units, find x.

Solution

(i) Perimeter $= 2(\text{Length}) + 2(\text{Width})$

$$= 2(3x + 11) + 2(5x - 23)$$
$$= 6x + 22 + 10x - 46$$
$$= 16x - 24$$

(ii) Perimeter $= 88$

Perimeter $= 16x - 24$

$88 = 16x - 24$

$88 + 24 = 16x$ (add 24 to both sides)

$112 = 16x$

$7 = x$ (divide both sides by 16)

Equations with fractions

If there are fractions in an equation, multiply all parts by a number that all of the denominators divide evenly into. This number is known as the common denominator.

Example

Solve the equation $\frac{1}{2}(7x - 2) + 5 = 2x + 7$.

Solution

$$\frac{1}{2}(7x - 2) + 5 = 2x + 7$$

$2\left(\frac{1}{2}(7x - 2)\right) + 2(5) = 2(2x) + 2(7)$	(multiply each term by 2)
$1(7x - 2) + 2(5) = 2(2x) + 2(7)$	(since $2 \times \frac{1}{2} = 1$)
$7x - 2 + 10 = 4x + 14$	(multiply out the brackets)
$7x + 8 = 4x + 14$	(simplify)
$7x + 8 - 4x = 4x + 14 - 4x$	(subtract $4x$ from both sides)
$3x + 8 = 14$	(simplify)
$3x + 8 - 8 = 14 - 8$	(subtract 8 from both sides)
$3x = 6$	(simplify)
$x = 2$	(divide both sides by 3)

key point

You cannot apply the method of multiplying all parts by a number unless the expression is an equation. That is, it must have an equals (=) sign.

Example

Solve the equation $\dfrac{x - 7}{2} = \dfrac{x + 3}{6}$.

Solution

$$\frac{x - 7}{2} = \frac{x + 3}{6}$$

$$6\left(\frac{x - 7}{2}\right) = 6\left(\frac{x + 3}{6}\right) \quad \text{(multiply each term by 6)}$$

$$3(x - 7) = 1(x + 3) \qquad \text{(divide the denominators into the LCM)}$$
$$3x - 21 = x + 3 \qquad \text{(multiply out the brackets)}$$
$$3x - 21 - x = x + 3 - x \qquad \text{(subtract } x \text{ from both sides)}$$
$$2x - 21 = 3 \qquad \text{(simplify)}$$
$$2x - 21 + 21 = 3 + 21 \qquad \text{(add 21 to both sides)}$$
$$2x = 24 \qquad \text{(simplify)}$$
$$x = 12 \qquad \text{(divide both sides by 2)}$$

Solve the equation $\dfrac{3(x + 3)}{4} - \dfrac{2(x - 3)}{3} = \dfrac{x + 1}{2}$.

Solution

$$\dfrac{3(x + 3)}{4} - \dfrac{2(x - 3)}{3} = \dfrac{x + 1}{2} \qquad \text{(the LCM of 4, 3 and 2 is 12)}$$

$$12\left(\dfrac{3(x + 3)}{4}\right) - 12\left(\dfrac{2(x - 3)}{3}\right) = 12\left(\dfrac{x + 1}{2}\right) \qquad \text{(multiply each term by the LCM, 12)}$$

$$3(3(x + 3)) - 4(2(x - 3)) = 6(x + 1) \qquad \text{(divide the denominators into the LCM)}$$

$$9(x + 3) - 8(x - 3) = 6(x + 1)$$

$$9x + 27 - 8x + 24 = 6x + 6 \qquad \text{(multiply out the brackets)}$$

$$x + 51 = 6x + 6 \qquad \text{(simplify)}$$

$$x + 51 - x = 6x + 6 - x \qquad \text{(subtract } x \text{ from both sides)}$$

$$51 = 5x + 6 \qquad \text{(simplify)}$$

$$51 - 6 = 5x + 6 - 6 \qquad \text{(subtract 6 from both sides)}$$

$$45 = 5x \qquad \text{(simplify)}$$

$$9 = x \qquad \text{(divide both sides by 5)}$$

(i) Express $\dfrac{2x - 1}{5} + \dfrac{x + 7}{2}$ as a single fraction.

Give your answer in its simplest form.

(ii) Hence or otherwise, solve the equation

$$\dfrac{2x - 1}{5} + \dfrac{x + 7}{2} = 6.$$

Solution

(i) $\dfrac{2x-1}{5} + \dfrac{x+7}{2}$ (common denominator is 10)

$\dfrac{2(2x-1) + 5(x+7)}{10}$

$\dfrac{4x-2+5x+35}{10}$

$\dfrac{9x+33}{10}$

(ii) $\dfrac{2x-1}{5} + \dfrac{x+7}{2} = 6$

$\dfrac{9x+33}{10} = 6$ (from **(i)**)

$10\left(\dfrac{9x+33}{10}\right) = 10(6)$ (multiply both sides by the LCM, 10)

$9x + 33 = 60$

$9x + 33 - 33 = 60 - 33$ (subtract 33 from both sides)

$9x = 27$ (simplify)

$x = 3$ (divide both sides by 9)

key point

We cannot multiply across by a number in part (i) because this expression is not an equation. Adding algebraic fractions was covered in an earlier chapter.

exam Q

The three angles of a triangle are $\dfrac{8(x-2)}{3}$, $4x + 7$, $\dfrac{5x-10}{2}$.

Find the value of x.

exam focus

Notice the link between Geometry and Algebra in this question.

Solution

The three angles of a triangle sum to 180°.

$\left(\dfrac{8(x-2)}{3}\right) + (4x+7) + \left(\dfrac{5x-10}{2}\right) = 180$

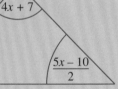

$6\left(\dfrac{8(x-2)}{3}\right) + 6(4x+7) + 6\left(\dfrac{5x-10}{2}\right) = 6(180)$ (multiply each term by the LCM, 6)

$2(8(x-2)) + 6(4x+7) + 3(5x-10) = 6(180)$ (divide the denominators into LCM)

$16(x-2) + 24x + 42 + 15x - 30 = 1\,080$ (multiply out the brackets)

$16x - 32 + 39x + 12 = 1\,080$ (simplify)

$55x - 20 = 1\,080$

$55x = 1\,100$ (add 20 to both sides)

$x = 20$ (divide both sides by 55)

aims
- ☐ To learn how to solve a quadratic equation when given in different forms
- ☐ To be able to solve quadratic equations when they appear during in-context questions

Any equation of the form $x^2 + bx + c = 0$ is called a quadratic equation. Solving a quadratic equation gives us the roots of the equation. These are the two values which satisfy the equation.

To solve a quadratic equation: factorise the expression then let each factor equal zero and solve.

key point

There are three different types of quadratic equation. It is vital for you to remember and be familiar with how to factorise each type. Methods of factorising were covered in an earlier chapter. It would be wise to revise these methods before continuing with this chapter.

Take out common terms	Difference of two squares	Factorise a trinomial
$x^2 + 2x = x(x + 2)$	$x^2 - 9 = (x + 3)(x - 3)$	$x^2 + 6x - 7 = (x - 1)(x + 7)$

Example

Solve the following quadratic equation: $2x^2 + 6x = 0$.

Solution

$$2x^2 + 6x = 0$$
$$2x(x + 3) = 0 \quad \text{(factorise: take out common factors)}$$
$$2x = 0 \quad \text{or} \quad x + 3 = 0 \quad \text{(let each factor equal zero)}$$
$$x = 0 \quad \text{or} \quad x = -3 \quad \text{(solve)}$$

key point

These values for x are called the roots of the quadratic equation. These values are the points where the graph of the quadratic function crosses the x-axis. This is covered in further detail in the chapter on graphing functions.

Example

Solve the following quadratic equation: $x^2 - 81 = 0$.

Solution

$$x^2 - 81 = 0$$
$$(x + 9)(x - 9) = 0 \quad \text{(factorise: difference of two squares)}$$
$$x + 9 = 0 \quad \text{or} \quad x - 9 = 0 \quad \text{(let each factor equal zero)}$$
$$x = -9 \text{ or} \quad x = 9 \quad \text{(solve)}$$

Example

Solve the following quadratic equation: $x^2 + 2x - 15 = 0$.

Solution

Factorise the quadratic trinomial on the left-hand side:

$x^2 + 2x - 15$ (final term, -15, is negative, so the signs in the brackets are different)

$(x + 5)(x - 3)$

Check: outside terms $= (x)(-3) = -3x$

inside terms $= (5)(x) \quad = \quad 5x$

sum $= \quad\quad\quad\quad\quad 2x =$ middle term of original quadratic trinomial

Therefore, factors $(x + 5)(x - 3)$ are correct.

$$x^2 + 2x - 15 = 0$$
$$(x + 5)(x - 3) = 0 \quad \text{(factorise: quadratic trinomial)}$$
$$x + 5 = 0 \quad \text{or} \quad x - 3 = 0 \quad \text{(let each factor equal zero)}$$
$$x = -5 \text{ or} \quad x = 3 \quad \text{(solve)}$$

It is a good idea to check your solutions in the original equation.
In this example:

$x = -5$: $(-5)^2 + 2(-5) - 15$	$x = 3$: $(3)^2 + 2(3) - 15$
$= 25 - 10 - 15$	$= 9 + 6 - 15$
$= 0$	$= 0$
$\therefore x = -5$ is a solution	$\therefore x = 3$ is a solution

Solve the following quadratic equations:

(i) $x^2 - 5x - 6 = 0$ (ii) $x^2 + 7x - 18 = 0$

Solution

(i) $x^2 - 5x - 6 = 0$

           $(x - 6)(x + 1) = 0$ (factorise: quadratic trinomial)

    $x - 6 = 0$ or $x + 1 = 0$

       $x = 6$ or $x = -1$

(ii) $x^2 + 7x - 18 = 0$

         $(x + 9)(x - 2) = 0$ (factorise)

   $x + 9 = 0$ or $x - 2 = 0$

     $x = -9$ or $x = 2$

Harry knows that: $(x - 2)(x + 8) = x^2 + 6x - 16$

Hence, or otherwise:

(i) Solve the equation $x^2 + 6x - 16 = 0$

(ii) Simplify $(x^2 + 6x - 16) \div (x - 2)$

Solution

(i) $x^2 + 6x - 16 = 0$

   $(x - 2)(x + 8) = 0$

    $x - 2 = 0$ and $x + 8 = 0$

       $x = 2$ and $x = -8$

(ii) $(x^2 + 6x - 16) \div (x - 2)$

$$= \frac{x^2 + 6x - 16}{x - 2}$$

$$= \frac{(x - 2)(x + 8)}{(x - 2)}$$

$$= x + 8$$

Remember, 'Hence' means that you can use the given information to solve the question.

Example

The sides of a right-angled triangle are $3x$, $4x$ and $5x$ in length. The area of the triangle is 216 square units. Use this information to write an equation in x.

Solve the equation and, hence, find the lengths of the sides of the triangle.

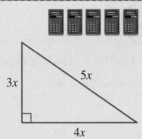

Solution

Area of a triangle $= \dfrac{1}{2}(\text{Base})(\perp \text{Height})$

$$216 = \dfrac{1}{2}(4x)(3x)$$

Write the formula and fill in the information from the question. Then solve the equation to find the remaining variable.

$2(216) = 2\left[\dfrac{1}{2}(4x)(3x)\right]$ (multiply both sides by 2)

$432 = 12x^2$

$\dfrac{432}{12} = x^2$ (divide both sides by 12)

$36 = x^2$

$0 = x^2 - 36$ (subtract 36 from both sides)

$0 = (x + 6)(x - 6)$ (factorise: difference of two squares)

$x + 6 = 0$ or $x - 6 = 0$ (let each factor equal zero)

$x = -6$	$x = 6$
Reject, as length can't be negative	Accept

If you get more than one answer it is important to look at which solutions make sense. Apply logic to determine which answers, if any, to reject.

Sides are: $3x = 3(6) = 18$ units

$4x = 4(6) = 24$ units

$5x = 5(6) = 30$ units

A car is moving away from a wall. The distance, S, in metres between the car and the wall, after t seconds, is given by:

$S = t^2 + 5t + 12.$

(i) How far is the car from the wall after 3 seconds?

(ii) How far is the car from the wall after 8 seconds?

(iii) After how many seconds is the car a distance of 48 m from the wall?

—Distance, S—

Solution

(i) Find S when $t = 3$: $S = t^2 + 5t + 12$

$S = (3)^2 + 5(3) + 12$

$S = 9 + 15 + 12 = 36$

Therefore, the car has travelled 36 m after 3 seconds.

(ii) Find S when $t = 8$: $S = t^2 + 5t + 12$

$S = (8)^2 + 5(8) + 12$

$S = 64 + 40 + 12 = 116$

Therefore, the car has travelled 116 m after 8 seconds.

(iii) Find t when $S = 48$:

$S = t^2 + 5t + 12$

$48 = t^2 + 5t + 12$

$48 - 48 = t^2 + 5t + 12 - 48$

$0 = t^2 + 5t - 36$

$0 = (t - 4)(t + 9)$ (factorise: quadratic trinomial)

$t - 4 = 0$ or $t + 9 = 0$

$t = 4$ or $t = -9$

Accept   Reject, as you can't have a negative time

Therefore, after 4 seconds the car is 48 m from the wall.

> **key point**
>
> This is also a functions question. These are covered in detail in the chapter on functions.

6 Simultaneous Equations

☐ To learn how to use suitable strategies for finding solutions to simultaneous linear equations with two unknowns

☐ To learn how to interpret the results from solving two equations simultaneously

Simultaneous linear equations with two unknowns

Simultaneous linear equations in two variables are solved with the following steps:

1. Write both equations in the form $ax + by = k$ and label the equations ① and ②.
2. Multiply one or both of the equations by a number in order to make the coefficients of x or y the same, but of opposite sign.
3. Add to remove the variable with equal coefficients but of opposite sign.
4. Solve the resultant equation to find the value of the remaining unknown (x or y).
5. Substitute this value in equation ① or ② to find the value of the other unknown.

Note: When there are two unknown variables we must have two equations.

Example

Solve the following pair of simultaneous equations:

$$2x + y = 72 \quad \text{and} \quad x - y = -27.$$

Solution

To eliminate the ys:

Step 1: ① $2x + y = 72$

② $\underline{x - y = -27}$ (add the rows)

Step 3: $3x = 45$ ($\div 3$)

Step 4: $x = 15$

To find the value for y, let $x = 15$ in either of the equations:

Step 5: ① $2x + y = 72$

$2(15) + y = 72$

$30 + y = 72$

$y = 42$

Therefore, the solution is $x = 15, y = 42$.

Note: Step 2 wasn't needed in this example.

Example

Solve the following pair of simultaneous equations:

$2p + 3q = 5$ and $p - 4q = -14$.

key point

Equations do not always have to be in terms of x and y.

Solution

To eliminate the ps:

Step 1: ① $2p + 3q = 5$
     ② $p - 4q = -14$ $(\times -2)$
     _____
Step 2: ① $2p + 3q = 5$
     ② $-2p + 8q = 28$ (add the rows)
     _____
Step 3: $11q = 33$ $(\div 11)$

Step 4: $q = 3$

Therefore, the solution is $p = -2, q = 3$.

To find the value for p, let $q = 3$ in either of the equations:

Step 5: ① $2p + 3q = 5$
     $2p + 3(3) = 5$
     $2p + 9 = 5$
     $2p = -4$
     $p = -2$

---

exam Q

Solve the following pair of simultaneous equations:

$5a + b = 1$ and $2a + 3b = -10$.

Solution

To eliminate the bs:

Step 1: ① $5a + b = 1$ $(\times -3)$
     ② $2a + 3b = -10$
Step 2: ① $-15a - 3b = -3$
     ② $2a + 3b = -10$ (add the rows)
Step 3: $-13a$ $= -13$ $(\div -13)$

Step 4: $a = 1$

Therefore, solution is $a = 1, b = -4$.

To find the value for b, let $a = 1$ in either of the equations:

Step 5: ① $5a + b = 1$
     $5(1) + b = 1$
     $5 + b = 1$
     $b = -4$

Solve the following pair of simultaneous equations:

$$3x + 5y = 13 \quad \text{and} \quad x + 2y = 5.$$

Solution

To eliminate the xs:

To find the value for x, let $y = 2$ in either of the equations:

Step 1: ① $\quad 3x + 5y = 13$

Step 5: ② $\quad x + 2y = 5$

② $\quad x + 2y = 5 \quad (\times -3)$

$x + 2(2) = 5$

Step 2: ① $\quad 3x + 5y = 13$

$x + 4 = 5$

② $-3x - 6y = -15 \quad$ (add the rows)

$x = 5 - 4$

Step 3: $\qquad -y = -2 \quad (\div -1)$

$x = 1$

Step 4: $\qquad y = 2$

Therefore, the solution is $x = 1$, $y = 2$.

Solve the following pair of simultaneous equations:

$$2p - 3q = 9 \quad \text{and} \quad 5p + 2q = 13.$$

key point

Sometimes it is necessary to multiply both rows by a number to get a variable to cancel.

Solution

To eliminate the qs:

To find the value for q, let $p = 3$ in either of the equations:

Step 1: ① $\quad 2p - 3q = 9 \quad (\times 2)$

Step 5: ② $\quad 5p + 2q = 13$

② $\quad 5p + 2q = 13 \quad (\times 3)$

$5(3) + 2q = 13$

Step 2: ① $\quad 4p - 6q = 18$

$15 + 2q = 13$

② $15p + 6q = 39 \quad$ (add the rows)

$2q = 13 - 15$

Step 3: $\qquad 19p = 57 \quad (\div 19)$

$2q = -2$

Step 4: $\qquad p = 3$

$q = -1$

Therefore, the solution is $p = 3$, $q = -1$.

(i) Solve the simultaneous equations $x + 2y = 4$ and $x - y = 1$.

(ii) By graphing the two lines on a single co-ordinate diagram, check your answer to part **(i)**.

Solution

(i) Solve the simultaneous equations:

Step 1: ① $x + 2y = 4$

       ② $x - y = 1$ ($\times 2$)

Step 2: ① $x + 2y = 4$

       ② $2x - 2y = 2$

Step 3: $3x = 6$ ($\div 3$)

Step 4: $x = 2$

Therefore, the solution is $x = 2$, $y = 1$.

To find the value for y, let $x = 2$ in either of the equations:

Step 5: ① $x + 2y = 4$

           $2 + 2y = 4$

           $2y = 4 - 2$

           $2y = 2$

           $y = 1$

(ii) To graph the lines, we need to find the points where they cross the x- and y-axes.

The process of graphing lines is covered in detail in the chapter on graphing functions and also the chapter on Coordinate Geometry of the Line in the *Less Stress More Success Maths Book 2*.

For $x + 2y = 4$:

On the x-axis, $y = 0$:

         $x + 2(0) = 4$

            $x = 4$

Line crosses x-axis at (4, 0).

On the y-axis, $x = 0$:

         $0 + 2y = 4$

           $2y = 4$

            $y = 2$

Line crosses y-axis at (0, 2).

For $x - y = 1$:

On the x-axis, $y = 0$:

         $x - 0 = 1$

            $x = 1$

Line crosses x-axis at (1, 0).

On the y-axis, $x = 0$:

         $0 - y = 1$

           $-y = 1$

            $y = -1$

Line crosses y-axis at (0, −1).

Graphing the lines:

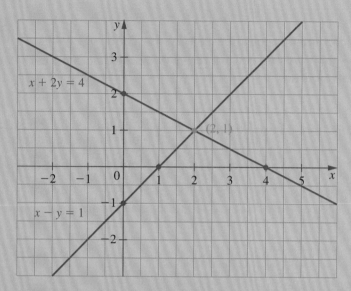

From the graph we can see that the point of intersection is (2,1). This agrees with the answer from part **(i)**.

Using simultaneous equations in real-world scenarios

Read the given information carefully and use it to form two equations. Then solve these equations simultaneously.

Suzanne is saving for Christmas. Throughout the year she collects savings stamps at the post office. By December she has €25 saved. This is made up of 20 cent saving stamps and 50 cent saving stamps. She has 104 saving stamps in total. Let x be the number of 20 cent saving stamps and y be the number of 50 cent saving stamps.

(i) Write an equation in x and y to represent the total number of stamps Suzanne has.

(ii) Write an equation in x and y to represent the total value of Suzanne's stamps.

(iii) Solve the equations to find the number of each type of stamp Suzanne has.

Solution

x = number of 20c stamps

y = number of 50c stamps

(i) Total number of stamps = $x + y$

$$104 = x + y$$

(ii) Value of stamps in cent = $20(x) + 50(y)$

$$2\,500 = 20x + 50y$$

$$250 = 2x + 5y$$

> **key point**
>
> Be aware that values were given here in both euro and cent. You must change to the same units before you begin the question.

(iii) Solve the equations:

Step 1: ① $x + y = 104$ $(\times -2)$

       ② $2x + 5y = 250$

Step 2: ① $-2x - 2y = -208$

       ② $2x + 5y = 250$

Step 3: $3y = 42$

Step 4: $y = 14$

Let $y = 14$:

Step 5: ① $x + y = 104$

          $x + 14 = 104$

              $x = 90$

Therefore, Suzanne has ninety 20c saving stamps and fourteen 50c saving stamps.

Example

Let the cost of a meal for an adult be €x and the cost of a meal for a child be €y. The cost of a meal for 3 adults and 2 children amounts to €125. The cost of a meal for 2 adults and 3 children amounts to €115.

(i) Write an equation in x and y to represent the cost of a meal for 3 adults and 2 children.

(ii) Write an equation in x and y to represent the cost of a meal for 2 adults and 3 children.

(iii) Solve these equations to find the cost of an adult's meal and the cost of a child's meal.

Solution

(i) The cost of a meal for 3 adults and 2 children amounts to €125: $3x + 2y = 125$.

(ii) The cost of a meal for 2 adults and 3 children amounts to €115: $2x + 3y = 115$.

(iii) Solving simultaneously:

Step 1: ① $\quad 3x + 2y = 125 \qquad (\times -3)$

        ② $\quad 2x + 3y = 115 \qquad (\times 2)$

Step 2: ① $\quad -9x - 6y = -375$

        ② $\quad 4x + 6y = 230$

Step 3: $\quad -5x \qquad\quad = -145 \quad (\div -5)$

Step 4: $\qquad\qquad x = 29$

Substitute $x = 29$ into one of the equations:

Step 5:

① $3(29) + 2y = 125$

$87 + 2y = 125$

$2y = 125 - 87$

$2y = 38$

$y = 19$

Therefore, an adult meal costs €29 and a child's meal costs €19.

The cost of five books and one magazine is €32.

The cost of eight books and three magazines is €54.

Let €b be the cost of a book and let €m be the cost of a magazine.

 (i) Write an equation in b and m to represent the cost of five books and one magazine.

 (ii) Write an equation in b and m to represent the cost of eight books and three magazines.

 (iii) Solve the equations to find the cost of a book and the cost of a magazine.

Solution

 (i) Five books + one magazine = 32

$$5b + m = 32$$

 (ii) Eight books and three magazines = 54

$$8b + 3m = 54$$

 (iii) Solve the equations:

Step 1: ① $\quad 5b + m = 32 \qquad (\times -3)$

        ② $\quad 8b + 3m = 54$

Step 2: ① $\quad -15b - 3m = -96$

        ② $\quad 8b + 3m = 54$

Step 3: $\qquad\quad -7b = -42 \quad (\div -7)$

Step 4: $\qquad\qquad\quad b = 6$

Let $b = 6$:

Step 5: ① $\quad 5b + m = 32$

$5(6) + m = 32$

$30 + m = 32$

$m = 32 - 30$

$m = 2$

Therefore, a book costs €6 and a magazine costs €2.

Example

An examination paper consists of 40 questions.

5 marks are given for each correct answer.

3 marks are deducted for each incorrect answer.

Kenny answered all 40 questions, getting x correct and getting y incorrect. His total score for the examination was 56 marks.

(i) Write an equation to represent the total number of questions Kenny answered.

(ii) Write an equation to represent the total number of marks Kenny scored.

(iii) Solve these equations to find how many questions Kenny answered correctly.

Solution

(i) Total number of questions $= x + y$

$$40 = x + y$$

(ii) Total marks $= 5(x) + (-3)(y)$

$$56 = 5x - 3y$$

(iii) Solve the equations:

Step 1: ① $\quad x + y = 40 \qquad (\times 3)$

$\qquad$ ② $5x - 3y = 56$

Step 2: ① $3x + 3y = 120$

$\qquad$ ② $5x - 3y = 56$

Step 3: $\qquad\qquad 8x = 176$

Step 4: $\qquad\qquad x = 22$

Let $x = 22$:

Step 5: ① $\quad x + y = 40$

$\qquad\qquad 22 + y = 40$

$\qquad\qquad\qquad y = 40 - 22$

$\qquad\qquad\qquad y = 18$

Therefore, Kenny answered 22 questions correctly and 18 questions incorrectly.

7 Long Division in Algebra

aims
☐ To learn how to divide algebraic expressions into one another
☐ To be able to use long division in algebra, where necessary, in solving in-context questions

Division in algebra follows the same procedure as division in arithmetic. Divide the numbers into the numbers and the algebraic parts into the algebraic parts.

The stages in dividing one algebraic expression by another are shown in the following example.

Example

Simplify.

(i) $\dfrac{-2x}{x}$ (ii) $\dfrac{24b}{8b}$ (iii) $\dfrac{-6p^2}{3p}$ (iv) $\dfrac{10a^2}{2a}$

Solution

(i) $\dfrac{-2x}{x} = \dfrac{(-2)(x)}{(1)(x)} = (-2)(1) = -2$ (-2 divided by 1 is -2.
                                                                   x divided by x is 1.)

(ii) $\dfrac{24b}{8b} = \dfrac{(24)(b)}{(8)(b)} = (3)(1) = 3$ (24 divided by 8 is 3.
                                                                   b divided by b is 1.)

(iii) $\dfrac{-6p^2}{3p} = \dfrac{(-6)(p)(p)}{(3)(p)} = (-2)(1)(p) = -2p$ (-6 divided by 3 is -2.
                                                                   p^2 divided by p is p.)

(iv) $\dfrac{10a^2}{2a} = \dfrac{(10)(a)(a)}{(2)(a)} = (5)(1)(a) = 5a$ (10 divided by 2 is 5.
                                                                   a^2 divided by a is a.)

key point

Divide the number on the top by the number on the bottom.
Divide the algebraic part on the top by the algebraic part on the bottom.

Dividing a quadratic expression by a linear expression

There are two methods for dividing a linear expression into a quadratic expression:

Method 1: Put the quadratic over the linear.

Factorise the quadratic.

Divide top and bottom by the linear expression.

Method 2: Follow the same procedure as long division in arithmetic.

The steps for this method are shown in the following example.

Example

Divide $x^2 + x - 12$ by $x + 4$.

Solution

Method 1: $\dfrac{x^2 + x - 12}{x + 4}$ $\quad$ (place the $x^2 + x - 12$ over the $x + 4$)

$\dfrac{(x + 4)(x - 3)}{x + 4}$ $\quad$ (factorise the top)

$\dfrac{\cancel{(x + 4)}(x - 3)}{\cancel{x + 4}}$ $\quad$ (divide top and bottom by $(x + 4)$)

$x - 3$

Method 2:

$$
\begin{array}{r}
x - 3 \\
x + 4 \enclose{longdiv}{x^2 + x - 12} \\
\end{array}
$$

$\quad$ ($x^2 \div x = x$, put x on top)

$x^2 + 4x \downarrow$ $\quad$ (multiply $x(x + 4) = x^2 + 4x$)

$-3x - 12$ $\quad$ (subtract bottom row from top and bring down -12)

$\quad$ ($-3x \div x = -3$, put -3 on top)

$-3x - 12$ $\quad$ (multiply $-3(x + 4) = -3x - 12$)

0 $\quad$ (subtract bottom row from the top)

Therefore, $(x^2 + x - 12) \div (x + 4) = x - 3$.

key point

Notice the importance of factorising here. Factorising is an important skill for you to have throughout your course.

Divide $x^2 - 3x - 10$ by $x + 2$.

Solution

Method 1: $\dfrac{x^2 - 3x - 10}{x + 2}$ (place the $x^2 - 3x - 10$ over the $x + 2$)

$\dfrac{(x + 2)(x - 5)}{x + 2}$ (factorise the top)

$x - 5$ (divide top and bottom by $x + 2$)

Method 2:

$$x + 2 \overline{\smash)\begin{array}{l} x - 5 \\ x^2 - 3x - 10 \end{array}}$$

(($x^2 \div x = x$, put x on top)

$\underline{x^2 + 2x} \quad \downarrow$ (multiply $x(x + 2) = x^2 + 2x$)

$-5x - 10$ (subtract bottom row from top and bring down -10)
                      ($-5x \div x = -5$, put -5 on top)

$\underline{-5x - 10}$ ($-5(x + 2) = -5x - 10$)

0 (subtract bottom row from the top row)

Therefore, $(x^2 - 3x - 10) \div (x + 2) = x - 5$.

Example

Divide $5x^2 + 13x + 6$ by $5x + 3$.

Solution

$$5x + 3 \overline{\smash)\begin{array}{l} x + 2 \\ 5x^2 + 13x + 6 \end{array}}$$

($5x^2 \div 5x = x$, put x on top)

$\underline{5x^2 + 3x} \quad \downarrow$ (multiply $x(5x + 3) = 5x^2 + 3x$)

$10x + 6$ (subtract bottom row from top and bring down $+6$)
                 ($10x \div 5x = 2$, put 2 on top)

$\underline{10x + 6}$ (multiply $2(5x + 3) = 10x + 6$)

0 (subtract bottom row from the top)

Therefore, $(5x^2 + 13x + 6) \div (5x + 3) = x + 2$.

Divide $6x^2 - x - 2$ by $3x - 2$.

Solution

$$
\begin{array}{r}
2x + 1 \\
3x - 2 \overline{\smash{\big)}\, 6x^2 - x - 2} \\
\underline{6x^2 - 4x} \downarrow \\
3x - 2 \\
\\
\underline{3x - 2} \\
0
\end{array}
$$

$(6x^2 \div 3x = 2x$, put $2x$ on top)

(multiply $2x(3x - 2) = 6x^2 - 4x$)

(subtract bottom row from the top and bring down -2)
($3x \div 3x = 1$, put 1 on top)

(multiply $1(3x - 2) = 3x - 2$)

(subtract bottom row from the top)

Therefore, $(6x^2 - x - 2) \div (3x - 2) = 2x + 1$.

The diagram shows a rectangular box.
It has a width of $2x - 1$.

Given that the area of the rectangle is $8x^2 + 6x - 5$, find the length of the rectangle.

Length

Width $= 2x - 1$

Solution

Area of a box = (Length)(Width)

$$
\frac{\text{Area of box}}{\text{Width}} = \text{Length} \quad \rightarrow \quad \frac{8x^2 + 6x - 5}{2x - 1} = \text{Length}
$$

Division:

$$
\begin{array}{r}
4x + 5 \\
2x - 1 \overline{\smash{\big)}\, 8x^2 + 6x - 5} \\
\underline{8x^2 - 4x} \downarrow \\
10x - 5 \\
\\
\underline{10x - 5} \\
0
\end{array}
$$

($8x^2 \div 2x = 4x$, put $4x$ on top)

(multiply $4x(2x - 1) = 8x^2 - 4x$)

(subtract bottom row from top and bring down -5)
($10x \div 2x = 5$, put 5 on top)

(subtract bottom row from top)

Therefore, length of the rectangle $= 4x + 5$.

8 Inequalities

The four inequality symbols are:

1. $>$ means greater than	**2.** $\geq$ means greater than or equal to
3. $<$ means less than	**4.** $\leq$ means less than or equal to

Algebraic expressions that are linked by one of the four inequality symbols are called **inequalities**. For example, $3x - 1 \geq 11$ and $-3 < 2x - 1 \leq 7$ are inequalities.

Solving inequalities is exactly the same as solving equations, with the following exception:

Multiplying or dividing both sides of an inequality by a negative number reverses the direction of the inequality symbol.

That is:

$>$ changes to $<$ $\geq$ changes to $\leq$

$<$ changes to $>$ $\leq$ changes to $\geq$

Solving an inequality means finding the values of x that make the inequality true.

The following rules apply to graphing inequalities on a number line:

Number line for $x \in \mathbb{N}$ or $x \in \mathbb{Z}$, use dots.	0 1 2
Number line for $x \in \mathbb{R}$, use a full heavy line.	2 3 4

Note: Inequalities can be turned around. For example:

$5 \leq x$ means the same as $x \geq 5$.

$8 \geq x \geq 3$ means the same as $3 \leq x \leq 8$.

It is vital that you are familiar with the basic **number systems**:

$\mathbb{N} = \{1, 2, 3, \ldots\}$, the set of natural numbers.

$\mathbb{Z} = \{\ldots -2, -1, 0, 1, 2, \ldots\}$, the set of integers.

$\mathbb{R} = $ all whole numbers, decimals, rational and irrational numbers are known as the set of real numbers.

(see booklet of formulae and tables)

(a) Graph the inequality $x \le 2$, $x \in \mathbb{R}$ on a number line.

(b) Put a tick (✓) in the correct box in the table to show which inequality is graphed on the number line below.

Inequality	Put a tick (✓) in **one** box only
$x \le 1, x \in \mathbb{N}$	
$x \ge 1, x \in \mathbb{N}$	
$x > 1, x \in \mathbb{N}$	
$x < 1, x \in \mathbb{N}$	

Solution

(a) As $x \in \mathbb{R}$, this is the set of real numbers less than or equal to 2.

Number line:

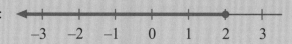

Note: 1. As $x \in \mathbb{R}$, we use full heavy shading on the number line.

2. A dot is put on 2 to indicate that it is included in the solution.

(b) From the number line:

We can see that the value for x is greater than, or equal to 1.

Inequality	Put a tick (✓) in **one** box only
$x \leq 1, x \in \mathbb{N}$	
$x \geq 1, x \in \mathbb{N}$	✓
$x > 1, x \in \mathbb{N}$	
$x < 1, x \in \mathbb{N}$	

Example

Graph on the number line the solution set of $2x + 1 < 9$, $x \in \mathbb{N}$.

Solution

$$2x + 1 < 9$$
$$2x + 1 - 1 < 9 - 1 \qquad \text{(subtract 1 from both sides)}$$
$$2x < 8 \qquad \text{(simplify)}$$
$$x < 4 \qquad \text{(divide both sides by 2)}$$

As $x \in \mathbb{N}$, this is the set of natural numbers less than 4.

Thus, the values of x are 1, 2 and 3.

Number line:

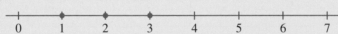

Note: As $x \in \mathbb{N}$, dots are used on the number line.

Example

Graph on the number line the solution set of $3x - 4 \geq 8, x \in \mathbb{Z}$.

Solution

$$3x - 4 \geq 8$$
$$3x - 4 + 4 \geq 8 + 4 \qquad \text{(add 4 to both sides)}$$
$$3x \geq 12 \qquad \text{(simplify)}$$
$$x \geq 4 \qquad \text{(divide both sides by 3)}$$

As $x \in \mathbb{Z}$, this is the set of natural numbers greater than or equal to 4.

Thus, the values of x are $4, 5, 6, 7, \ldots$

Number line:

Note: As $x \in \mathbb{Z}$, dots are used on the number line.

Students often have difficulty determining the correct region for the final answer. Spend some time practising this.

Find the values of x for which $4x - 1 < 11$, $x \in \mathbb{N}$.

Solution

$4x - 1 < 11$

$4x - 1 + 1 < 11 + 1$ (add 1 to both sides)

$4x < 12$

$x < 3$ (divide both sides by 3)

Since $x \in \mathbb{N}$, x is a positive whole number, which must be less than 3.

Therefore, $x = 1$ or 2.

Example

Graph on the number line the solution set of $2x - 1 > 9$, $x \in \mathbb{Z}$.

Solution

$2x - 1 > 9$

$2x > 9 + 1$ (add 1 to both sides)

$2x > 10$ (simplify)

$x > 5$ (divide both sides by 2)

As $x \in \mathbb{Z}$, this is the set of integers (whole numbers) greater than 5.

Thus, the values of x are 6, 7, 8, 9, 10, etc.

Number line:

Note: As $x \in \mathbb{Z}$, dots are used on the number line.

Example

(i) Find the solution set P of $3x + 8 \leq 14$, $x \in \mathbb{R}$.

(ii) Find the solution set Q of $5 - 2x < 11$, $x \in \mathbb{R}$.

(iii) Find $P \cap Q$ and graph your solution on the number line.

Solution

We solve each inequality separately and then combine the solutions.

(i) P: $3x + 8 \leq 14$

$3x \leq 6$

$x \leq 2$

(ii) Q: $5 - 2x < 11$

$5 - 11 < 2x$

$-6 < 2x$

$-3 < x$

So $x > -3$.

(iii) Combining the two inequalities gives:

$P \cap Q$: $\quad -3 < x \leq 2, \qquad x \in \mathbb{R}$

This is the set of positive and negative real numbers between -3 and 2, including 2 but not including -3.

Number line:

We were not asked to draw the number lines in parts (i) and (ii), but as you can see from below, these number lines are helpful when plotting the final solution set:

(i) $P: x \leq 2$
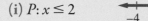
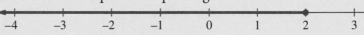

(ii) $Q: x > -3$

$P \cap Q: -3 < x \leq 2$
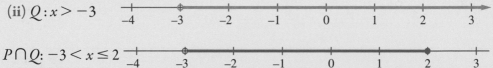

Note: 1. As $x \in \mathbb{R}$, we use full heavy shading on the number line.

2. A hollow circle is put around -3 to indicate that it is **not** included in the solution.

3. A dot is put on 2 to indicate that it **is** included in the solution.

In-context questions

The following questions involve the use of inequalities in real-world situations.

The students in a class run a race.

(a) It takes Ali 14·8 seconds to run the race.

   (i) Plot the point 14·8 on the number line below.

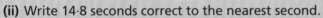

      12   13   14   15   16   17   18

   (ii) Write 14·8 seconds correct to the nearest second.

(b) Fill in the missing description and graph in the table below. In each case, $t \in \mathbb{R}$.

	Description	Graph ($t \in \mathbb{R}$)
1.	t is greater than 12	10 11 12 13 14 15 16 17 18 (open circle at 12, shaded right)
2.	t is _____	10 11 12 13 14 15 16 17 18 (open circle at 15, shaded left)
3.	t is between 12 and 17	10 11 12 13 14 15 16 17 18

(c) It takes Ben 12·1 seconds to run the race.
It takes Ciara 11 seconds to run the race.
Which one of these numbers is a natural number ($\mathbb{N}$)? Give a reason for your answer.

Solution

(a) (i) 14·8 will be $\dfrac{4}{5}$ of the way from 14 to 15. Indicated by the red dot below:

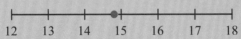

      12   13   14   15   16   17   18

   (ii) To round 14·8, we look at the number after the decimal point. Since this number is 8, which is ≥ 5, we round up the number before the decimal point. Answer: 15 seconds.

(b) For graph 2, we can see that the shading is starting at 15 (but not including 15) and moving towards the smaller side.
So we complete the description as follows:

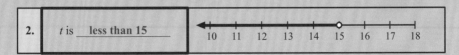

2.	t is less than 15	10 11 12 13 14 15 16 17 18 (open circle at 15, shaded left)

For graph 3, we need to shade in the region between the numbers 12 and 17 but since the 12 and 17 are not included, we put an open circle on each of these numbers and shade the region between them.

3.	t is between 12 and 17	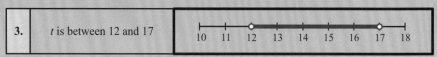

(c) A natural number is a positive whole number, so 11 is the natural number.

The width of a rectangle is x cm and its length is $(2x - 3)$ cm, where $x \in \mathbb{N}$.

(i) Find an expression, in terms of x, for the perimeter of the rectangle.

(ii) If the perimeter of the rectangle must be greater than 42 cm, find the smallest possible value of x.

(iii) Hence, find the area of the rectangle for this value of x.

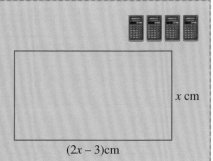

$(2x - 3)$cm

Solution

(i) Perimeter = 2(Length) + 2(Width)

$$= 2(2x - 3) + 2(x)$$
$$= 4x - 6 + 2x$$
$$= 6x - 6$$

(ii) Perimeter > 42

$\quad 6x - 6 > 42 \qquad$ (from **(i)**)

$\quad\quad\quad 6x > 48$

$\quad\quad\quad\quad x > 8$ cm

Therefore, the smallest possible value of x is 9 cm, since $x \in \mathbb{N}$.

(iii) If $x = 9$:

Width = 9   and   Length = 2(9) − 3 = 15

Area = Length × Width

$$= 9 \times 15$$
$$= 135 \text{ cm}^2$$

aims

- ☐ To become familiar with the rules of indices
- ☐ To learn how to use the rules of indices to solve problems
- ☐ To understand index notation
- ☐ To be able to work with index notation when solving problems

In the expression a^m, a is the base and m is the index.

The index can also be called the power or the exponent.

key point

a^m is read as 'a to the power of m'.

Example

Using the calculator or otherwise, evaluate:

(i) 8^4 (ii) 12^3 (iii) 3^6

Solution

(i) $8^4 = 8 \times 8 \times 8 \times 8 = 4\,096$

(ii) $12^3 = 12 \times 12 \times 12 = 1\,728$

(iii) $3^6 = 3 \times 3 \times 3 \times 3 \times 3 \times 3 = 729$

key point

If the power is very large, it is quicker and easier to use the power button on the calculator: $\boxed{x^\blacksquare}$ or $\boxed{y^\blacksquare}$

Example: 6^9 can be entered as $\boxed{6}$ $\boxed{x^\blacksquare}$ $\boxed{9}$ $\boxed{=}$ 10077696

exam Q

The table below shows the values when 2 is raised to certain powers.

(i) Complete the table.

Power of 2	Expanded power of 2	Answer
2^1	2	2
2^2	2 × 2	4
2^3	2 × 2 × 2	
2^4		
2^5		
2^6		
2^7		
2^8		
2^9		

(ii) Maria wins a prize in a lottery and is given two options.

Option A: €1 000 cash today

Option B: Take €2 today, €4 tomorrow, €8 the next day and doubling every day for 9 days.

Which option should Maria choose if she wants to get the most prize money? Explain your answer.

Solution

(i) Completed table:

Power of 2	Expanded power of 2	Answer
2^1	2	2
2^2	2 × 2	4
2^3	2 × 2 × 2	8
2^4	2 × 2 × 2 × 2	16
2^5	2 × 2 × 2 × 2 × 2	32
2^6	2 × 2 × 2 × 2 × 2 × 2	64
2^7	2 × 2 × 2 × 2 × 2 × 2 × 2	128
2^8	2 × 2 × 2 × 2 × 2 × 2 × 2 × 2	256
2^9	2 × 2 × 2 × 2 × 2 × 2 × 2 × 2 × 2	512

(ii) Option A: €1 000 now

Option B: €2 + €4 + €8 + €16 + €32 + €64 + €128 + €256 + €512 = €1 022

Maria should choose option B because it will give her €22 more than option A.

Rules of Indices	
Where $a \in \mathbb{R};\ p, q \in \mathbb{Q};\ a \neq 0$:	
Rules (see booklet of formulae and tables).	**Example**
1. $a^p a^q = a^{p+q}$	$5^4 5^3 = 5^{4+3} = 5^7$ $x^3 x^5 = x^{3+5} = x^8$
2. $\dfrac{a^p}{a^q} = a^{p-q}$	$\dfrac{3^5}{3^2} = 3^{5-2} = 3^3$ $\dfrac{x^7}{x^3} = x^{7-3} = x^4$
3. $(a^p)^q = a^{pq}$	$(3^2)^4 = 3^8$ $(x^3)^4 = x^{12}$

Example

(i) Write $a^4 \times a^3$ in the form a^n, where $n \in \mathbb{N}$.

(ii) Hence or otherwise, evaluate $2^4 \times 2^3$.

Solution

(i) $a^4 \times a^3 = a^{4+3} = a^7$ (use rule: $a^p a^q = a^{p+q}$)

(ii) $2^4 \times 2^3 = 2^7 = 128$ (use calculator to evaluate 2^7)

Example

(i) Write $\dfrac{p^7}{p^3}$ in the form p^n, where $n \in \mathbb{N}$.

(ii) Hence or otherwise, evaluate $\dfrac{11^7}{11^3}$.

Solution

(i) $\dfrac{p^7}{p^3} = p^{7-3} = p^4$ (use rule: $\dfrac{a^p}{a^q} = a^{p-q}$)

(ii) $\dfrac{11^7}{11^3} = 11^4 = 14\,641$ (use calculator to evaluate 11^4)

Example

(i) Write $(r^3)^2$ in the form r^n, where $n \in \mathbb{N}$.

(ii) Hence or otherwise, evaluate $(5^3)^2$.

Solution

(i) $(r^3)^2 = r^{3 \times 2} = r^6$ (use rule: $(a^p)^q = a^{pq}$)

(ii) $(5^3)^2 = 5^6 = 15\,625$ (use calculator to evaluate 5^6)

Find the exact value of $(4^2)^3$.

Solution

Method 1: Using rules of indices: $(4^2)^3$

     $4^{2 \times 3}$ (use rule: $(a^p)^q = a^{pq}$)

     4^6 (simplify)

     $4\,096$ (use calculator to evaluate 4^6)

Method 2: Using the calculator: $(4^2)^3$

     $(16)^3$ (use calculator to evaluate 4^2)

     $4\,096$ (use calculator to evaluate 16^3)

Simplify $(a^3 \times a \times a^4)^2$.

Solution

$(a^3 \times a \times a^4)^2$

$(a^3 \times a^1 \times a^4)^2$

$(a^{3+1+4})^2$ (use rule: $a^p a^q = a^{p+q}$)

$(a^8)^2$ (simplify)

$a^{8 \times 2}$ (use rule: $(a^p)^q = a^{pq}$)

a^{16}

Example

Evaluate $36^{\frac{1}{2}}$.

Solution

Using the calculator: $36^{\frac{1}{2}} = 6$.

A special index: $a^{\frac{1}{2}} = \sqrt{a}$

Example: $16^{\frac{1}{2}} = \sqrt{16} = 4$

Example

Evaluate $25^{\frac{1}{2}}$.

Solution

$25^{\frac{1}{2}} = \sqrt{25} = 5$

Example

Simplify $\dfrac{a^9 \times a^3}{a^6 \times a^2}$. Give your answer in the form a^n, where $n \in \mathbb{N}$.

Solution

$\dfrac{a^9 \times a^3}{a^6 \times a^2}$

$\dfrac{a^{9+3}}{a^{6+2}}$　　　　　(use rule: $a^p a^q = a^{p+q}$)

$\dfrac{a^{12}}{a^8}$　　　　　(simplify the powers)

a^{12-8}　　　　　(use rule: $\dfrac{a^p}{a^q} = a^{p-q}$)

a^4　　　　　(simplify the powers)

(i) Simplify $\dfrac{b^5 \times b^2}{b \times b^3}$. Give your answer in the form b^n, where $n \in \mathbb{N}$.

(ii) Using your answer to part **(i)**, or otherwise, find the value of $\dfrac{6^5 \times 6^2}{6 \times 6^3}$.

Solution

(i) $\dfrac{b^5 \times b^2}{b \times b^3}$ $\qquad\qquad (b = b^1)$

$\dfrac{b^{5+2}}{b^{1+3}}$ $\qquad\qquad$ (use rule: $a^p a^q = a^{p+q}$)

$\dfrac{b^7}{b^4}$ $\qquad\qquad$ (simplify the powers)

b^{7-4} $\qquad\qquad$ (use rule: $\dfrac{a^p}{a^q} = a^{p-q}$)

b^3 $\qquad\qquad$ (simplify the powers)

(ii) $\dfrac{6^5 \times 6^2}{6 \times 6^3} = 6^3$ $\qquad\qquad$ (from part **(i)**, replacing b with 6)

$= 216$

Index notation

When dealing with very large or very small numbers it can be easier to perform calculations if the numbers are expressed in what is known as 'index notation' or 'scientific notation'. This means to express the numbers in the form $a \times 10^n$, where $1 \leq a < 10$ and $n \in \mathbb{Z}$.

- $1\,200 = 1{\cdot}2 \times 1\,000 = 1{\cdot}2 \times 10^3$
- $35\,400\,000 = 3{\cdot}54 \times 10\,000\,000 = 3{\cdot}54 \times 10^7$

The natural display calculators can be very useful when working in index notation. But remember to show your steps or full marks may not be awarded.

It is very important that you know how to put your calculator into scientific mode and be able to enter data that is in index notation.

CASIO	SHARP
Put your calculator into scientific mode:	Put your calculator into scientific mode:
SHIFT then SETUP	Set up
7 : Sci	1 : FSE
	1 : SCI
Select a number between 0 and 9. This is the number of significant figures the calculator will display. Selecting 9 will be fine.	Select a number between 0 and 9. This is the number of significant figures the calculator will display. Selecting 9 will be fine.
To enter 6.7×10^{-15} press the following buttons:	To enter 6.7×10^{-15} press the following buttons:

CASIO: 6 · 7 ×10ˣ (−) 1 5

SHARP: 6 · 7 Exp (−) 1 5

Example

Write 6 300 in the form $a \times 10^n$, where $1 \le a < 10$ and $n \in \mathbb{N}$.

Solution

Method 1: 6 300
$$= 6.3 \times 1\,000$$
$$= 6.3 \times 10^3$$

Method 2: Put your calculator into scientific mode, type in 6 300 and press the equal button.
$$= 6.3 \times 10^3$$

Express 2^{24} in the form $a \times 10^n$, where $1 \leq a < 10$ and $n \in \mathbb{N}$, correct to three significant figures.

Solution

Method 1: Use your calculator to find the value of 2^{24}.

$2^{24} = 16\ 777\ 216$ (on calculator display)

$2^{24} = 1 \cdot 6777216 \times 10\ 000\ 000$

$2^{24} = 1 \cdot 6777216 \times 10^7$

$2^{24} = 1 \cdot 6800000 \times 10^7$ (to three significant figures)

$2^{24} = 1 \cdot 68 \times 10^7$

Method 2: Put your calculator into scientific mode. Enter 2^{24} and press the equal button:

$1 \cdot 6777216 \times 10^7$ (on calculator display)

$1 \cdot 6800000 \times 10^7$ (to three significant figures)

$1 \cdot 68 \times 10^7$

The diameters of Venus and Saturn are $1 \cdot 21 \times 10^4$ km and $1 \cdot 21 \times 10^5$ km. What is the difference between the diameters of the two planets? Give your answer in the form of $a \times 10^n$, where $n \in \mathbb{Z}$ and $1 \leq a < 10$.

Solution

Start by putting your calculator into scientific mode.

Difference in diameters = Diameter of Saturn − Diameter of Venus

Difference in diameters = $1 \cdot 21 \times 10^5 - 1 \cdot 21 \times 10^4$

Difference in diameters = $1 \cdot 089 \times 10^5$ km

10 Pattern

aims

☐ To recognise a repeating pattern and to make predictions from that pattern

☐ To represent patterns with tables, diagrams and graphs

☐ To generate and write expressions and formulae from patterns for particular terms in a sequence

☐ To know about linear, quadratic and exponential patterns

☐ To understand and be able to carry out the operation called differencing

An introduction to pattern

key point

A pattern always has a logical sequence.

Examples of pattern in everyday life:

1. Traffic lights: Green, Amber, Red, Green, Amber, . . .
2. Weekdays: M, T, W, T, F, M, T, W, . . .
3. Tidal movements: High tide, Low tide, High tide, Low tide, . . .
4. Notes of the scale: doh, ray, me, fah, so, la, ti, doh, ray, . . .

Sequences

A sequence is a particular order in which related things follow each other. For example:

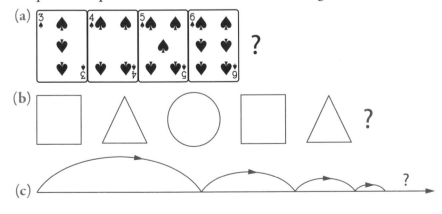

(a)

(b)

(c)

(d) 1, 3, 6, 10, ?

- The first term of a sequence is called T_1, the second term is T_2 and so on.
- To predict what will come next in a sequence, we must find a rule that links one number or diagram with the next.

In our course we study three main types of numeric sequences and their associated graphs.

1. **Linear sequences**, e.g. 2, 5, 8, 11, 14, ...

   A linear (arithmetic) sequence is formed by adding/subtracting the same amount to any term to get the next term. This 'same amount' is usually called the **common difference**, d.

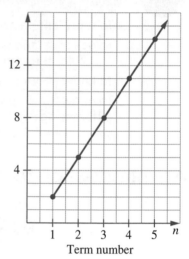

2. **Quadratic sequences**, e.g. 0, 5, 8, 9, 8, 5, 0

   Sequences that have an nth term containing n^2 as the highest power are called quadratic sequences. We use a technique called differencing, explained later in this chapter, when working with quadratic sequences.

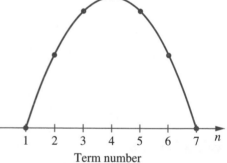

3. **Exponential sequences**, e.g. 2, 4, 8, 16, ...

   In these sequences, when we look for a term-to-term rule, we find that it involves multiplying (by 2 in this case).

   When terms are calculated by multiplying, the sequence is always exponential.

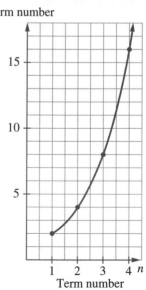

Predicting the pattern

Aspects of mathematics are about pattern. The following questions are simple and numeric.

exam Q

Find the next three terms in each sequence.

(i) 2, 5, 8, _____, _____, _____

(ii) 16, 12, 8, _____, _____, _____

(iii) 1, 4, 9, 16, _____, _____, _____

key point

A sequence in which you go from term to term by adding (or subtracting) the same number each time is called an arithmetic sequence or linear sequence.

Solution

(i) 2, 5, 8, . . .

(ii) 16, 12, 8, . . .

key point

Arithmetic sequence with common difference −4.

(iii) 1, 4, 9, 16, . . .

$(1)^2, (2)^2, (3)^2, (4)^2, (5)^2, (6)^2, (7)^2$

1,   4,   9, 16, 25, 36, 49

key point

A much tougher question: this is not an arithmetic sequence. Some outside-the-box thinking makes the solution simple. It is in fact a quadratic sequence.

exam focus

This question was very badly answered by candidates. It was awarded a total of 5 marks for all nine correct answers. However, it is important to note that 3 of those marks were awarded for **any one** of those nine correct answers.

exam
Q

In a number pyramid you add the two numbers in the lower blocks to find the number in the block above (for examples, 2 + 3 = 5).

Complete the number pyramid by filling in the empty spaces.

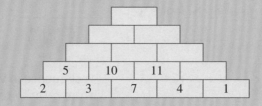

Solution

First

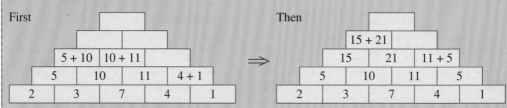

5 + 10	10 + 11		
5	10	11	4 + 1
2	3	7	4	1

$\Rightarrow$

Then

15 + 21		
15	21	11 + 5
5	10	11	5
2	3	7	4	1

Finally

	73	
36		37
15	21	16
5	10	11	5
2	3	7	4	1

exam
focus

This question was extremely badly answered by candidates. As a result it was awarded only 5 marks for all seven correct answers. However, it is important to note that 3 of those marks were awarded for **any one** of those seven correct answers.

exam
Q

Kevin has saved €20. He gets €7 a week for doing jobs at home.
He spends €2 on sweets every week and saves the rest in a piggybank.

(i) How much money has he saved at the end of week 1?

(ii) Complete the table to show how his savings grow in the first five weeks.

Start	Week 1	Week 2	Week 3	Week 4	Week 5
€20		€30			

(iii) Write down a formula (in words) to represent the amount he has saved at the end of each week.

(iv) Kevin would like to buy a mobile phone costing €100. Use your formula to find out how many weeks he needs to save to have enough money to buy the phone.

(v) Kevin stops buying the sweets after five weeks. How much can he save each week after that?

(vi) Kevin thinks he can buy his phone three weeks sooner with the extra savings. Do you agree with Kevin? Explain your answer.

Solution

(i) $20 + 7 - 2 = 20 + 5 = $ €25 saved at end of week 1

(ii)

20	= 20
20 + 5	= 25
20 + 5 + 5	= 30
20 + 5 + 5 + 5	= 35
20 + 5 + 5 + 5 + 5	= 40
20 + 5 + 5 + 5 + 5 + 5	= 45

exam focus

However, the examiner also accepted an answer of €5 saved in part **(i)**.

Start	Week 1	Week 2	Week 3	Week 4	Week 5
€20	€25	€30	€35	€40	€45

(iii)   €20 plus €5 for each week

= €20 + €5 multiplied by the week number

= €20 + €5n, where n is the week number

= 20 + 5n

(iv)   20 + 5n = 100   (an equation in disguise)

$5n = 100 - 20$ (subtract 20 from both sides)

$5n = 80$

$n = 16$ (divide both sides by 5)

After 16 weeks of saving, Kevin has enough money to buy the phone.

(v) Sweets cost Kevin €2 each week. If he stops buying sweets he has an extra €2 to save. €5 + €2 = €7.

(vi) In 13 weeks he saves

$20 + (5 + 5 + 5 + 5 + 5) + (7 + 7 + 7 + 7 + 7 + 7 + 7 + 7)$

= 20 + five (5) + eight (7)

= 20 + 25   + 56

= € 101   yes agree with Kevin.
The above work is my explanation.

key point

3 weeks sooner is (16 − 3) = 13 weeks

exam focus

This question was awarded a total of 24 marks.

As candidates found part **(iii)** and part **(vi)** very difficult, each part was awarded only 2 marks.

Candidates did better on parts **(i)**, **(ii)**, **(iv)** and **(v)**. These four parts were awarded 5 marks each.

It is vital that you attempt each part of every question in this exam.

Predicting pattern from given graphs and diagrams

Not all patterns are numeric. For example, a series of shapes are made using matches.

How many matches will be needed for the 6th shape?

Answer: 5, 9, 13, 17, 21 then 25 matches for the 6th shape, that is four extra matches each time.

Three experiments on temperature are done in the science lab.
Pupils record and plot the temperature of each experiment
each hour, for five hours.

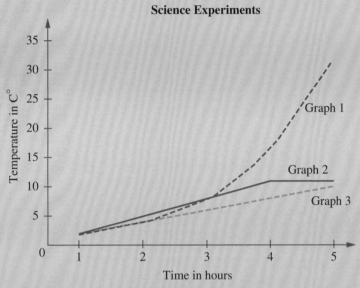

In experiment A, the temperature doubles every hour.

In experiment B, the temperature increases by 2° every hour.

In experiment C, the temperature increases by 3° each hour for three hours and
then remains constant.

Identify each experiment by its number.

Solution

In experiment B the temperature increases by +2° every hour. This is what we call
a linear (straight line) sequence. Hence, B is associated with graph 3.

Experiment C is also linear but stops increasing after three hours.
Hence, C is associated with graph 2.

By elimination, A is associated with graph 1.

Graph 1 is exponential
(more on this later in
the chapter).

5 marks were awarded for matching the letters A, B, C, with the correct
positions.

Remember to attempt everything.

Melissa bought a horse in 2007 for €500. She took the horse to the sales each year for three years to have it valued but did not sell. She recorded the values on the graph below.

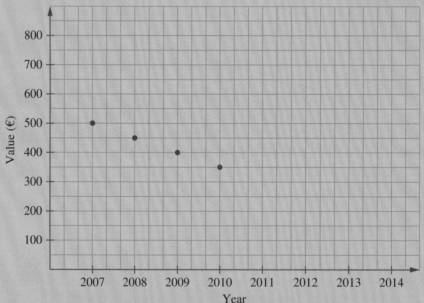

(i) Use a line to join the points on the graph.

(ii) If the pattern continued, what was the horse worth in 2011?

(iii) How much does the horse lose in value each year?

(iv) Melissa will sell the horse when it reaches a value of €200. If the pattern continues, in what year will she sell the horse?

(v) James bought a horse for €700 in 2007. His horse loses value at a constant rate. It was worth €100 in 2011. Mark these two points on the graph above, and join them with a straight line.

(vi) In what year will the two horses have the same value? What is that value?

(vii) Louise examines the graph and says 'looking at the slopes of the lines, I can tell which horse loses value faster'. Explain in your own words what Louise means.

This question links pattern and coordinate geometry.

Solution

(i)

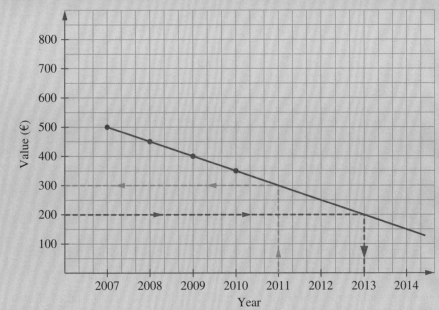

Year

(ii) €300 (reading from the graph ---▶---)

(iii) 500, 450, 400, 350 . . . suggests minus €50 each year.

(iv) The horse is worth €200 in 2013 (reading from the graph ---▶---)

Full marks awarded for answers in the range €275 to €325.

(v)

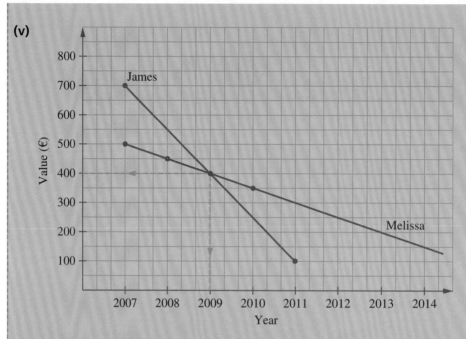

(vi) Reading from the graph above, the two horses have the same value in 2009 and that value was €400.

The point of intersection of the two lines gives the answers to part **(vi)**.

(vii) The (downward) slope of Melissa's line tells Louise that the value of Melissa's horse is decreasing. However, the much steeper (downward) slope of James's line tells Louise that the value of his horse is decreasing at a faster rate.

This question was awarded a total of 29 marks.
The very easy part **(i)** was awarded 2 marks.
The badly answered part (vii) was also awarded 2 marks.
Parts **(ii), (iii), (iv), (v)** and **(vi)** were awarded 5 marks each.

Example

In the following pattern, the first figure represents 1 dot, the second represents 3 dots, etc.

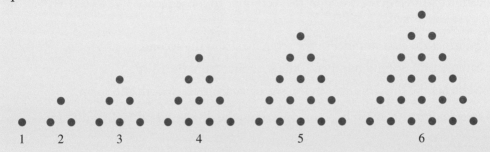

This pattern can also be described in function notation:

$f(1) = 1,$ $f(2) = 3,$ $f(3) = 6$, etc.

(i) Hence or otherwise, write down:

   (a) $f(4)$ (b) $f(6)$ (c) $f(7)$ (d) $f(8)$

(ii) Write down the value of q where $f(q) = 55$.

Solution

(i) From the diagram we construct the following table.

Figure	1	2	3	4	5	6	7	8	9	10
Number of dots	1	3	6	10	15	21	28	36	45	55

Notice:

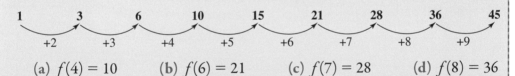

   (a) $f(4) = 10$ (b) $f(6) = 21$ (c) $f(7) = 28$ (d) $f(8) = 36$

(ii) By observation from the table constructed in part (i):

   $f(10) = 55,$ which means $q = 10.$

exam focus

Exam questions will often link topics, as above where pattern is linked with function notation.

Differencing (change)

Many investigative and problem-solving questions lead to a sequence of numbers. The technique of differencing is useful in certain situations involving sequences. To observe an application of differencing, we apply the technique to the sequence $3, 7, 13, 21, 31, 43, \ldots$ To find the first difference:

- Subtract the first number in the sequence from the second.
- Subtract the second number in the sequence from the third.
- Subtract the third number in the sequence from the fourth and so on.

The second differences can be found by taking the difference of the first differences. Hence, we find:

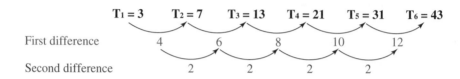

	$T_1 = 3$	$T_2 = 7$	$T_3 = 13$	$T_4 = 21$	$T_5 = 31$	$T_6 = 43$
First difference		4	6	8	10	12
Second difference			2	2	2	2

Linear patterns

- When the first difference is the same value each time, the pattern is referred to as a **linear pattern**. A linear pattern is formed by adding/subtracting the same amount to any term to get the next term. When graphed, a linear pattern is a straight line.

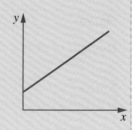

- When the first difference is not the same value each time, the pattern is non-linear.

Quadratic patterns

- When the second difference is the same value each time, the pattern is referred to as a **quadratic pattern**. When graphed, a quadratic pattern will be a curve and not a straight line.

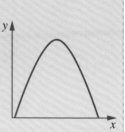

- When the second difference is not same value each time, the pattern is not a quadratic pattern.

Camille uses sticks to make a sequence of patterns.
The first 3 patterns in her sequence are
shown below.

(a) Draw Pattern 4 in the sequence.

Pattern 1   Pattern 2   Pattern 3

(b) Fill in the table below to show
the number of triangles in each of the first five patterns.
One is already done for you.

Pattern	1	2	3	4	5
No. of triangles		3			

(c) What kind of sequence is made by the number of triangles in each pattern?
Give a reason for your answer.

(d) One pattern has exactly 21 triangles. Tick the correct box to show which
pattern this is.
Show your working out

The pattern with 21 triangles is: Pattern 11   Pattern 21   Pattern 41
(tick (✓) **one** box only)   ☐   ☐   ☐

(e) There are also parallelograms in these patterns. The number of parallelograms
in Pattern n is: $n^2 - n$
Use this to work out the number of parallelograms in Pattern 30 (when $n = 30$).

Solution

(a) To form pattern 4, we need to add two triangles onto the side of pattern 3.

(b) The number of triangles is increasing by two each pattern. Complete the table as:

Pattern	1	2	3	4	5
No. of triangles	1	3	5	7	9

(c) The sequence of the number of triangles is:

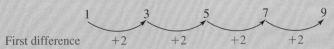

First difference   +2   +2   +2   +2

Since all of the first differences are the same, the sequence is linear.

(d) The pattern starts with 1 triangle and grows by 2 triangles each time.
Number of triangles per pattern: 1, 3, 5, 7, 9, 11, 13, 15, 17, 19, 21, 23, …
So, the pattern with 21 triangles would be the 11th pattern.

Pattern 11	Pattern 21	Pattern 41
✓	☐	☐

(e) Number of parallelograms $= n^2 - n$ (let $n = 30$)

$$= (30)^2 - (30)$$
$$= 900 - 30$$
$$= 870$$

Sometimes a question can look difficult, but has a simple solution.

Example

A stone is dropped from the top of a building and lands on the ground below. The total distance that it fell from the top of the building was recorded at 1- second intervals. It landed on the ground after 5 seconds.
The results are shown in the table.

Time (seconds)	Distance (metres)
0	0
1	6
2	24
3	54
4	96
5	150

(i) What is the height of the building?

(ii) Do these results form a linear relationship? Explain your answer.

(iii) Could these results be represented by a quadratic function? Explain your answer.

Solution

(i) 150 m (since the stone landed on the ground after 5 seconds and it had fallen 150 m).

(ii) and (iii)

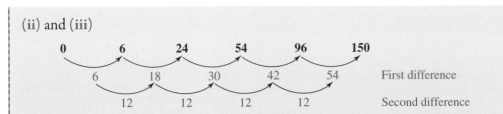

0		6		24		54		96		150
	6		18		30		42		54	First difference
		12		12		12		12		Second difference

Not linear, as the first differences are not constant. However, since the second difference is constant, it is quadratic.

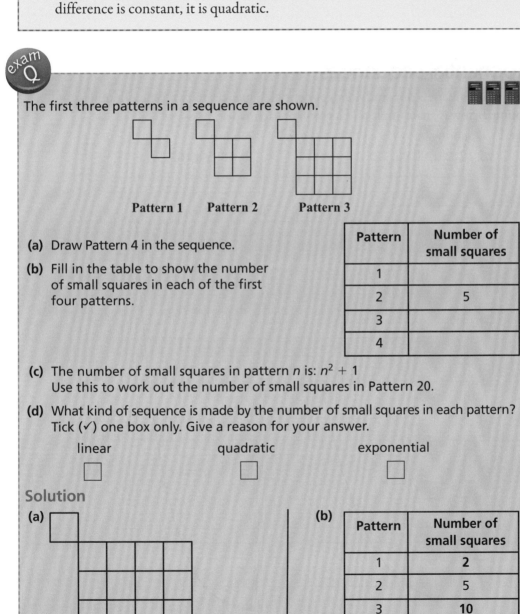

exam Q

The first three patterns in a sequence are shown.

Pattern 1   Pattern 2   Pattern 3

(a) Draw Pattern 4 in the sequence.

(b) Fill in the table to show the number of small squares in each of the first four patterns.

Pattern	Number of small squares
1	
2	5
3	
4	

(c) The number of small squares in pattern n is: $n^2 + 1$
Use this to work out the number of small squares in Pattern 20.

(d) What kind of sequence is made by the number of small squares in each pattern?
Tick (✓) one box only. Give a reason for your answer.

linear ☐   quadratic ☐   exponential ☐

Solution

(a)

(b)

Pattern	Number of small squares
1	2
2	5
3	10
4	17

(c) Number of small squares = $n^2 + 1$
Number of small squares = $(20)^2 + 1$
Number of small squares = $400 + 1$
Number of small squares = 401

(d) The formula has an n^2 in it, so the sequence is quadratic.

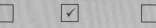

linear   quadratic   exponential

☐   ✓   ☐

Exponential sequences

The syllabus restricts our study of exponential sequences to two types: doubling and trebling. Below is an example and a graph of each type.

Type 1   Doubling
      6, 12, 24, 48, 96, . . .

Type 2   Trebling
      2, 6, 18, 54, 162, . . .

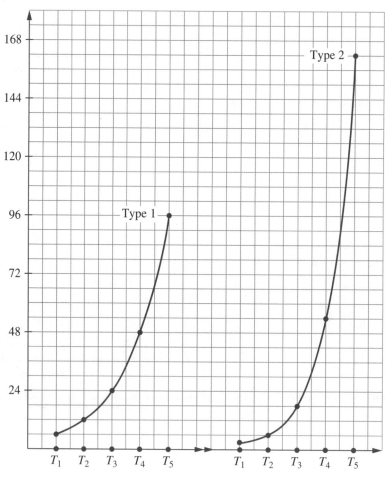

key point

Exponent is another word for power, e.g. 3^1, 3^2, 3^3, 3^4, ... In everyday language exponential growth is used to indicate very rapid growth.

Remember: exponent = power = index

exam Q

Given the right conditions of food, moisture and warmth, some bacteria can divide into two every hour. This is known as binary fission and is especially important in the food industry in order to avoid food poisoning. The diagram below shows the growth by division of one bacterium.

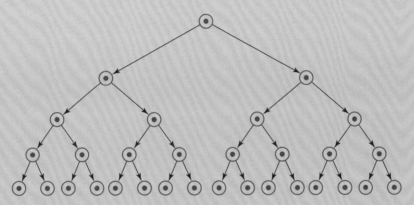

(i) How many bacteria will this single one have become after growing for five hours?

(ii) Complete this table.

Time in hours	0	1	2	3	4	5	6	7
Number of bacteria	2^0	2^1			2^4			

(iii) By noting $2^0 = 1$; $2^1 = 2$; $2^2 = 4$; $2^3 = 8$; etc.

Draw the graph in the domain $0 \leq t \leq 7$, where t is the time in hours.

(iv) Use your graph to estimate the number of bacteria present after $5\frac{1}{2}$ hours.

(v) Use the table of results from part (ii) to write down an expression for the number of bacteria present after one day.

Solution

(i) After five hours there are $2^5 = 2 \times 2 \times 2 \times 2 \times 2 = 32$ bacteria.

(ii)

Time in hours	0	1	2	3	4	5	6	7
Number of bacteria	2^0	2^1	2^2	2^3	2^4	2^5	2^6	2^7

(iii)

Time in hours	0	1	2	3	4	5	6	7
Number of bacteria	1	2	4	8	16	32	64	128

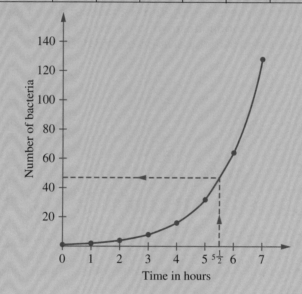

(iv) From the above graph we follow ↑ and estimate that there are 47 bacteria after $5\frac{1}{2}$ hours.

(v) After 24 hours there are 2^{24} bacteria $= 16\,777\,216$.

key point

1 day = 24 hours

11 Sets

aims

- [ ] To be familiar with set symbols and set notation
- [ ] To be able to construct and interpret Venn diagrams
- [ ] To know the meaning of terms such as subsets, cardinal number, set difference and complement of a set
- [ ] To be able to identify whether the commutative property holds in situations involving sets
- [ ] To gain the necessary skills to solve problems concerning two sets
- [ ] To be able to apply sets in the many different topics where it may be examined, e.g. probability, number theory

Basic revision of sets terminology

1. A set is a well-defined collection of objects.

   The set of whole numbers between $2\frac{1}{4}$ and $5\frac{1}{3}$ is a well-defined set, but for the example the set of good actors is not. Different people will give different answers.

2. Equal sets

   Two sets are equal if they contain exactly the same elements.

   If $E = \{1, 3, 8, 9\}$ and $F = \{9, 3, 1, 8\}$, then $E = F$.

3. Element of a set.

   If $E = \{$The first five letters in the alphabet$\}$, then

   (i) d is an element of E and is written as $d \in E$

   (ii) y is not an element of E and is written as $y \notin E$

4. The universal set (U)

   The set from which all other sets being considered is called the universal set, U.

5. If every element of a set E is also an element of a set F, then E is said to be a subset of F. This is written as $E \subset F$.

6. Union of two sets $(E \cup F)$

   The union of two sets is found by putting together in a new set all the elements of E and F without repeating an element. It is written as $E \cup F$.
   If $E = \{b, p, q, y\}$ and $F = \{a, b, e, y\}$, then
   $E \cup F = \{a, b, e, p, q, y\}$.

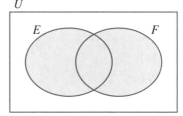

When listing the elements of a set, place the elements between chain brackets { } and separate them with commas. An element is never repeated and the order of the elements is **not** important.

7. Intersection of two sets $(E \cap F)$

The intersection of two sets E and F is the set of elements that are in **both** E and F.

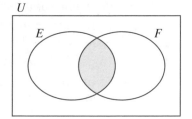

8. The complement of a set (E')

The complement of a set E is the set of elements in the universal set U which are **not** in E.

It is written as E'.

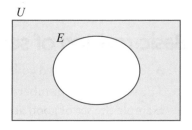

Some set notation is given in the booklet of formulae and tables, which is available to you in the examination.

exam Q

The Venn diagram represents the sets:

Natural numbers $\mathbb{N}$

Integers $\mathbb{Z}$

Rational numbers $\mathbb{Q}$

(i) Enter the following numbers in the correct sections of the Venn diagram.

(a) 4

(b) –3

(c) 0

(d) $\dfrac{10}{3}$

(e) –7·9

(f) –25

(ii) Hence or otherwise, shade the empty set.

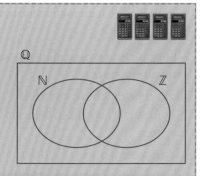

Solution

Using the number sets in the booklet of formulae and tables or from the chapter on number systems we write:

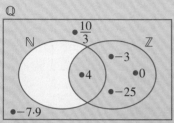

The set $\mathbb{N}$ is a subset of the set $\mathbb{Z}$.
It is written as $\mathbb{N} \subset \mathbb{Z}$, similarly $\mathbb{Z} \subset \mathbb{Q}$ and $\mathbb{N} \subset \mathbb{Q}$.

This question links sets and number systems.

$A = \{p, q, r\}$

Write down a subset of A that has: **(i)** one element **(ii)** two elements.

Solution

$A = \{p, q, r\}$

(i) Subsets of A that have one element are:

    $\{p\}$ or $\{q\}$ or $\{r\}$ (any one will do).

(ii) Subsets of A that have two elements are:

    $\{p, q\}$ or $\{p, r\}$ or $\{q, r\}$ (any one will do).

Set difference

To illustrate set difference, we consider two sets
E and F where

$E = \{a, b, p, q, x, y\}$ and $F = \{a, b, c, d\}$.

If we remove from set E all the elements which are
in set F, we have E less F.

E less F is denoted by $E \backslash F$.

We then write $E \backslash F = \{p, q, x, y\}$.

$E \backslash F$ is the set of elements of E which are not in F.

We may illustrate set difference by Venn diagrams as follows:

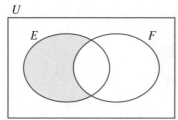

Shaded area is $E \backslash F$

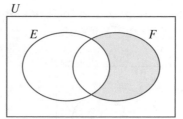

Shaded area is $F \backslash E$

Example

From the Venn diagram list the elements of:

(a) $R \cup S$ (b) $S \cup R$

(c) $R \backslash S$ (d) $S \backslash R$

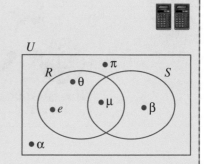

Solution

(a) $R \cup S = \{e, \theta, \mu, \beta\}$

(b) $S \cup R = \{\beta, \mu, e, \theta\}$

(c) $R \backslash S = \{e, \theta\}$

(d) $S \backslash R = \{\beta\}$

The cardinal number of a set (#)

The number of elements in a set is called the cardinal number of the set.

The symbol # is used to denote cardinal number.

If $E = \{p, q, r, s\}$,   then $\# E = 4$.

Example

From the given Venn diagram, answer the following:

(i) A (ii) A'

(iii) $\#A$ (iv) $\#A'$

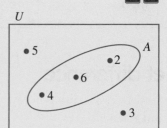

Solution

(i) $A = \{4, 6, 2\}$ (ii) $A' = \{5, 3\}$

(iii) $\#A = 3$ (iv) $\#A' = 2$

key point

Recall that A', the complement of A, is all elements **not** in A.

Example

In the given Venn diagram, each dot represents an element. Write down:

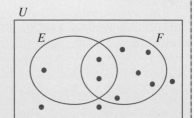

(i) #E   (ii) #$(E \cap F)$

(iii) #$(F \backslash E)$ (iv) #F'

(v) #$[U \backslash (E \cup F)]$ (vi) #$[(F \backslash E) \cup (E \backslash F)]$

Solution

(i) #$E = 3$ (ii) #$(E \cap F) = 2$

(iii) #$(F \backslash E) = 5$ (iv) #$F' = 4$

(v) #$[U \backslash (E \cup F)] = \#[(E \cup F)'] = 3$

(vi)

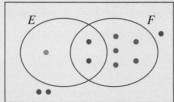

$$\#[(F \backslash E) \cup (E \backslash F)] = 6$$

Numerical problems on two sets

If some of the elements are not in any of the given sets, then we must introduce the universal set. Also, in many problems we may have to use a variable, say, x, to represent the number of elements in a region.

In numerical problems on sets:

the symbol $\cap$ means **and**

the symbol $\cup$ means **or**.

The sports played by a set of girls *G* and a set of boys *B* in a Limerick school are shown in the Venn diagram.

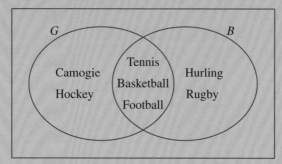

(i) Describe the region of the diagram where camogie and hockey are located.

(ii) Describe the region of the diagram where tennis, basketball and football are located.

(iii)(a) In the Venn diagram, shade the set $A \cup B$.

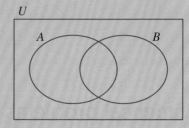

(b) In the Venn diagram, shade the set $(A \cup B)'$, where $(A \cup B)'$ is the complement of $A \cup B$.

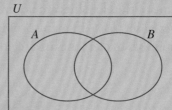

This question was awarded a total of 25 marks, with 10 of those marks awarded for the very easy and well answered part **(ii)**. Remember to attempt every part of every question, and write **something** down . . . you never know how marks will be awarded!

Solution

(i) Girls only or $G \setminus B$ or $U \setminus B$.

(ii) $G \cap B$ or sports played by both girls and boys.

(iii) (a) U **(b)** U

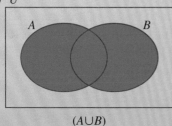   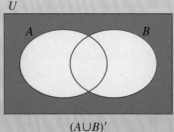

             $(A \cup B)$ $(A \cup B)'$

key point

Unfortunately, candidates mixed up $A \cup B$ and $A \cap B$. Be sure you know the difference between A union B and A intersection B.

exam Q

The universal set $U = \{1, 2, 3, 4, 5, 7, 10, 11, 13, 17, 19, 20\}$.

A is the set of prime numbers between 1 and 20. B is the set of factors of 20.

(i) List the elements of the set A.

    $A = \{$,   ,   ,   ,   ,   ,   , $\}$

(ii) List the elements of the set B.

    $B = \{$,   ,   ,   ,   , $\}$

(iii) Fill in the Venn diagram below, placing all elements of U in the correct regions.

U

(iv) List the elements of $A \cap B$.

   $A \cap B = \{$ $\}$

(v) Complete the sentence below.

   If an element is in the region $A \cap B$, it has two properties: it is a prime number and it is _____.

(vi) The number 16 is added to the universal set. Place 16 in the correct region in the Venn diagram in part **(iii)** and explain why you placed it there.

Solution

(i) $A = \{2, 3, 5, 7, 11, 13, 17, 19\}$

(ii) $B = \{1, 2, 4, 5, 10, 20\}$

(iii)

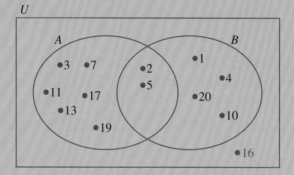

(iv) $A \cap B = \{2, 5\}$

(v) If an element is in the region $A \cap B$, it has two properties: it is a prime number and it is a factor of 20.

(vi) 16 (in red colour above in the Venn diagram) is not a prime number and is not a factor of 20. It is outside $A \cup B$ but is in U.

Many candidates mixed up union ($\cup$) and intersection ($\cap$).

This question was awarded a total of 24 marks, with generous marks (partial credit) for any correct work. Parts **(i)** + **(v)** were each awarded 2 marks and parts **(ii)**, **(iii)**, **(iv)** and **(vi)** each awarded 5 marks.

A school team orders t-shirts and half zips.
Jill, Mike, Ted, and Gary order t-shirts (*T*).
Jill and Alice order half zips (*Z*).
Ben and Zena don't order either.

(a) Complete the Venn diagram below to show this
   information, where:
   U is the whole team (the universal set)
   T is the set of people ordering t-shirts
   Z is the set of people ordering half zips.

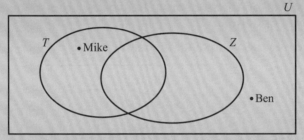

(b) In total, how many students are on the team?

(c) Write each term from the following list into the correct space in the table
   below, to match each description to the correct term in set notation. *Z'* is the
   complement of *Z*.

$$Z \setminus T \qquad T \cap Z \qquad Z'$$

	Description	Set Notation
1	The students who order **both** t-shirts **and** half zips	
2	The students who order half zips but **not** t-shirts	
3	The students who do **not** order half zips	

Solution

(a) Jill ordered both, so she goes into the middle.
   Ben and Zena didn't order either, so they go outside of the two sets.

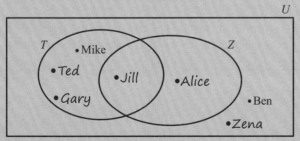

(b) Total number of students = 7

(c)

	Description	Set Notation
1	The students who order **both** t-shirts **and** half zips	$T \cap Z$
2	The students who order half zips but **not** t-shirts	$Z \setminus T$
3	The students who do **not** order half zips	Z'

Kate carried out a survey on the students in her year (U) to see how many study French (F) or German (G).

Her results are shown in the Venn diagram below, where $x \in \mathbb{N}$.

(a) How many students study German but not French?

(b) In total, how many students study French? Give your answer in terms of x.

(c) Complete the sentence correctly:

'$3x$ students study [   ].'

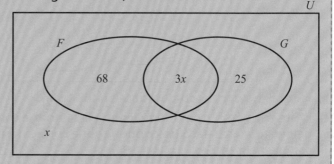

(d) Explain what the following statement means, in the context of Kate's survey:
$\#(F \setminus G) = 68$

(e) One student is picked at random from the $3x + 25$ students who study German. Write down the probability that this student also studies French. Give your answer as a fraction, in terms of x.

(f) Kate finds out that there are 141 students in total in her year. She writes the following equation in x:
$$68 + 3x + 25 + x = 141$$
Work out the value of x.

Solution

(a) 25 students study German but not French (shaded in orange below)

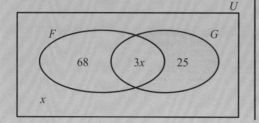

(b) $(68 + 3x)$ students study French (shaded in green below)

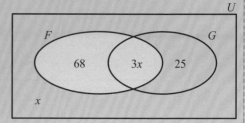

(c) From the Venn diagram we can see that the 3x is in the intersection of the two sets. So, we can complete the sentence as:

'3x students study | both French and German | .'

(d) #(F\G) = 68 means that 68 students study French but not German (this means that they study French only)

(e) Out of the 3x + 25 who study German, 3x of them study French too.

$$P(\text{Study French from the group that study German}) = \frac{3x}{3x + 25}$$

(f) 68 + 3x + 25 + x = 141

$$93 + 4x = 141 \qquad \text{(simplifying like terms)}$$
$$4x = 141 - 93 \qquad \text{(subtracting 93 from both sides)}$$
$$4x = 48$$
$$x = 12 \qquad \text{(dividing both sides by 4)}$$

In a survey of 30 students in a class it was found that:

21 own a mobile phone (M) and 11 own a computer (C).
6 own both a mobile phone and a computer.

(i) Represent this information in the Venn diagram below.

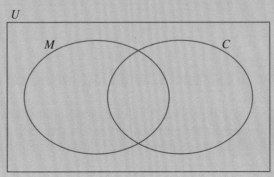

(ii) A student is selected at random from the class. What is the probability that the student owns:

   (a) A computer

   (b) A mobile phone but not a computer

   (c) Neither a mobile phone nor a computer?

Solution

(i)

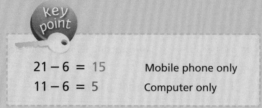

$$21 - 6 = 15 \qquad \text{Mobile phone only}$$
$$11 - 6 = 5 \qquad \text{Computer only}$$

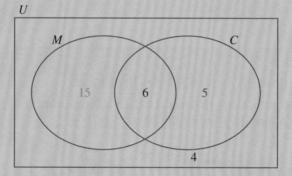

Finally, $15 + 6 + 5 = 26$. With 30 students in the class, we state 4 have neither.

(ii)

   (a) P (Student has a computer) $= \dfrac{11}{30}$

   (b) P (Student has a mobile phone but not a computer) $= \dfrac{15}{30} = \dfrac{1}{2}$

   (c) P (Student has neither) $= \dfrac{4}{30} = \dfrac{2}{15}$.

This question links sets and probability. A more detailed study of these types of questions on probability may be found in the chapter on probability in *Less Stress More Success Junior Cycle Maths Book 2*.

- ☐ To learn what a function is and how to recognise one
- ☐ To become familiar with the notation associated with functions
- ☐ To be able to solve problems involving functions

A function is a rule that changes one number (input) into another number (output). Functions are often represented by the letters f, g, h or k. We can think of a function, f, as a number machine which changes an input, x, into an output, $f(x)$.

Input

Output

$f(x)$, which denotes the output, is read as 'f of x'.

key point

A function is also called a **mapping** or simply a **map**.

For example, let's represent the function 'double input and then add 5' by the letter f. This can be written as:

$$f:x \rightarrow 2x + 5 \quad \text{or} \quad f(x) = 2x + 5 \quad \text{or} \quad y = 2x + 5$$

$$(\text{input, output}) = (x, f(x)) = (x, 2x + 5) = (x, y)$$

One number is mapped onto another number.
In the above example, x is mapped onto $2x + 5$, usually written as $f: x \rightarrow 2x + 5$.

A function connects every input (x) in the domain to an output $(f(x))$ in the range.

A function is another way of writing an algebraic formula that links input (x) to output $(f(x))$.

key point

Note the different notations for function:

$f: x \rightarrow$

$f(x)$

y

Types of functions	
Linear	$f: x \rightarrow ax$ or $f: x \rightarrow ax + b$
Quadratic	$f: x \rightarrow ax^2 + bx + c$
Exponential	$f: x \rightarrow ab^x$

Input number

If $f: x \rightarrow 2x + 5$, then $f(3)$ means 'input 3 into the function', i.e. it is the result of applying the function f to the number 3.

$$f(3) = 2(3) + 5 = 6 + 5 = 11 \qquad (\text{input} = 3, \text{output} = 11)$$
$$(\text{input, output}) = (3, f(3)) = (3, 11)$$

A function performs the exact same procedure to each input number and produces only one output number for each input number.

The set of input numbers is called the **domain**. The set of output numbers is called the **range**.

The set of **all possible outputs** is called the **codomain**.

In general, the range is a subset of the codomain. However, sometimes the range and the codomain are the same.

Consider the function f shown:

$f = \{(1, a), (2, b), (3, d), (4, d)\}$

from set X to set Y.

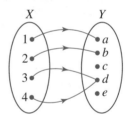

Domain: The set of elements from which the arrows leave: $\{1, 2, 3, 4\}$.
Range: The set of elements where the arrows arrive: $\{a, b, d\}$.
Codomain: The **possible** set of elements into which the arrows go: $\{a, b, c, d, e\}$.

Example

$P = \{(1, 5), (2, 8), (2, 9), (3, 10)\}$

Write out the domain and range of P.

Solution

The domain is the inputs:	Domain $= \{1, 2, 2, 3\}$
	Domain $= \{1, 2, 3\}$ (do not enter 2 twice)
The range is the outputs:	Range $= \{5, 8, 9, 10\}$

$T = \{(1, p), (2, p), (3, q), (4, r)\}$

Write out the domain and range of T.

Solution

The domain is the inputs: Domain = {1, 2, 3, 4}

The range is the outputs: Range = {p, p, q, r}

                                   Range = {p, q, r}   (do not enter p twice)

To recognise if a mapping represents a function:

- If any element in the domain has no arrow, then it is **not** a function.
- If any element in the domain has more than one arrow leaving it, it is **not** a function.
- Therefore, a mapping represents a function if there is **exactly one arrow leaving every element in the domain**.

Example

State whether each of the following mapping diagrams is a function.
Give a reason for your answer in each case.

(i) 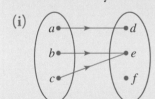   (ii)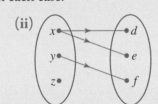

(iii) 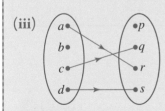   (iv)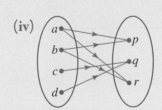

Solution

(i) Is a function, as each element of the domain (inputs) has only one output.

(ii) Is not a function, as input x has two outputs. Also, input z has no output.

(iii) Is not a function, as one element in the domain, input b, has no output.

(iv) Is not a function, as inputs a and b have more than one output.

Example

Find the value of $f(-3)$ when $f(x) = 2 - 5x$.

Solution

$$f(x) = 2 - 5x$$
$$f(-3) = 2 - 5(-3)$$
$$f(-3) = 2 + 15$$
$$f(-3) = 17$$

key point

Substituting and solving equations are vital skills for you to have when working with functions. Working with functions follows the same procedure as substituting and solving equations in Algebra. These were covered in earlier chapters.

Example

A function is given by $f(x) = 2x - 1$. Find the value of $f(2) + f(-1)$.

Solution

$$f(x) = 2x - 1$$
$$f(2) = 2(2) - 1 \qquad\qquad f(-1) = 2(-1) - 1$$
$$f(2) = 4 - 1 \qquad\qquad f(-1) = -2 - 1$$
$$f(2) = 3 \qquad\qquad f(-1) = -3$$

Therefore, $f(2) + f(-1) = 3 + (-3)$
$$f(2) + f(-1) = 3 - 3$$
$$f(2) + f(-1) = 0$$

exam Q

$f(x) = 3x - 5$. Find the value of:

(i) $f(7)$ (ii) $f(-2)$

Solution

(i) $f(x) = 3x - 5$

$f(7) = 3(7) - 5$

$f(7) = 21 - 5$

$f(7) = 16$

(ii) $f(x) = 3x - 5$

$f(-2) = 3(-2) - 5$

$f(-2) = -6 - 5$

$f(-2) = -11$

exam Q

$f(x) = x^2 + x - 3$. Find the value of.

(i) $f(3)$ (ii) $f(-1)$

Solution

(i) $f(x) = x^2 + x - 3$

$f(3) = (3)^2 + (3) - 3$

$f(3) = 9 + 3 - 3$

$f(3) = 9$

(ii) $f(x) = x^2 + x - 3$

$f(-1) = (-1)^2 + (-1) - 3$

$f(-1) = 1 - 1 - 3$

$f(-1) = -3$

Example

A function is given by $f(x) = 4x - 3$. If $f(x) = 21$, find x.

Solution

$f(x) = 4x - 3$

$21 = 4x - 3$ (let $f(x) = 21$)

$21 + 3 = 4x - 3 + 3$ (add 3 to both sides)

$24 = 4x$ (simplify)

$\dfrac{24}{4} = x$ (divide both sides by 4)

$6 = x$

Example

A function f is defined as $f(x) = 3x - 2$.
Find the missing numbers, p, q and r.

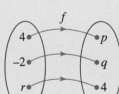

Solution

$$f(x) = 3x - 2$$
$$f(4) = 3(4) - 2$$
$$p = 12 - 2$$
$$\therefore \quad p = 10$$

$$f(x) = 3x - 2$$
$$f(-2) = 3(-2) - 2$$
$$q = -6 - 2$$
$$\therefore \quad q = -8$$

To find r, we are given an equation in disguise
Output $= 4$, find input r:

$$f(x) = 3x - 2$$
$$f(r) = 3r - 2$$
$$4 = 3r - 2$$
$$4 + 2 = 3r - 2 + 2$$
$$6 = 3r$$
$$2 = r$$

A mapping diagram of the function $g(x) = x^2$, is shown below.

(a) Fill in the 4 missing entries in the diagram.

(b) Write down the range of the function $g(x)$, as shown in the diagram.

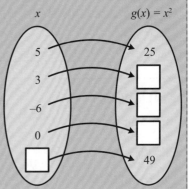

Solution

(a)
$$g(x) = x^2$$
$$g(3) = (3)^2$$
$$g(3) = 9$$

$$g(x) = x^2$$
$$g(-6) = (-6)^2$$
$$g(-6) = 36$$

$$g(x) = x^2$$
$$g(0) = (0)^2$$
$$g(0) = 0$$

$$g(x) = x^2 \quad \text{Completed mapping:}$$
$$49 = x^2$$
$$\sqrt{49} = x$$
$$7 = x$$

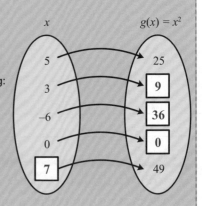

(b) The range is the list of output values, so range $= \{25, 9, 36, 0, 49\}$

A school is planning a trip to a local museum. They are taking the school's mini-bus. It will cost €42 for parking for the bus during the day. Tickets to enter the museum are €16·50 per student.

(i) Find the total cost of the trip in terms of n, where n equals the number of students who go on the trip.

(ii) Find the total cost of the trip for 20 students.

(iii) Find the cost of the trip, per student, if 14 students go on the trip.

(iv) If the total cost of the trip came to €339, how many students went on the trip?

key point

Notice that this is actually a fairly straightforward pattern question.

Solution

(i) n = Number of students

Cost = Cost of parking + Ticket per student

$C = €42 + €16·50(n)$

(ii) Find the cost when $n = 20$: $C = €42 + €16·50(n)$

$$C = €42 + €16·50(20)$$
$$C = €42 + €330$$
$$C = €372$$

Therefore, the trip will cost €372 for a group of 20 students.

(iii) Find the cost when $n = 14$: $C = €42 + €16·50(n)$

$$C = €42 + €16·50(14)$$
$$C = €42 + €231$$
$$C = €273$$

Therefore, the trip will cost €273 for a group of 14 students.

Cost per person = €273 ÷ 14 = €19·50 per person

(iv) Find n when $C = 339$:
$$C = €42 + €16·50(n)$$
$$€339 = €42 + €16·50(n)$$
$$339 - 42 = 16·50(n)$$
$$297 = 16·50(n) \qquad (÷ 16·50)$$
$$18 = n$$

Therefore, 18 students went on the trip.

A ball is thrown into the air from the roof of a building. Its height above the ground, h (measured in metres), at any given time after the ball is thrown, t (measured in seconds), can be modelled using the quadratic function $h = -4t^2 + 20t + 23$.

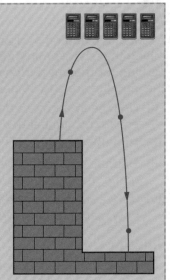

(i) Find the height of the ball above the ground after 3 seconds.

(ii) Find the two times when the height of the ball is 39 m.

(iii) Find the height of the building.

Solution

(i) Find h when $t = 3$: $h = -4t^2 + 20t + 23$

$$h = -4(3)^2 + 20(3) + 23$$
$$h = -4(9) + 60 + 23$$
$$h = -36 + 83$$
$$h = 47$$

Therefore, after 3 seconds, the ball was at a height of 47 m.

(ii) Find t when $h = 39$ m:

$$h = -4t^2 + 20t + 23$$
$$39 = -4t^2 + 20t + 23$$
$$4t^2 - 20t - 23 + 39 = 0$$
$$4t^2 - 20t + 16 = 0 \qquad \text{(divide both sides by 4)}$$
$$t^2 - 5t + 4 = 0$$
$$(t - 4)(t - 1) = 0$$

$t - 4 = 0$ or $t - 1 = 0$

$t = 4\,\text{sec}$ $t = 1\,\text{sec}$

Therefore, after 1 second the ball is at a height of 39 m and it is again at this height after 4 seconds.

(iii) The ball is released when time is 0 seconds.

Find h when $t = 0$: $h = -4t^2 + 20t + 23$

$$h = -4(0)^2 + 20(0) + 23$$
$$h = -4(0) + 0 + 23$$
$$h = 0 + 23$$
$$h = 23$$

The ball is at height 23 m when it is released, therefore the height of the building was 23 m.

13 Graphing Functions

□ To be able to graph functions of various forms
□ To be able to use the graphs to find the solution to given questions

Graphing functions

To graph a function, find points which satisfy the function by substituting values in for x and finding the corresponding y-values. Plot these points and join them up to obtain the graph of the function.

To better understand the graphs of functions, you should practise graphing functions on a graphing calculator or graphing software, such as Geogebra (free to download from www.geogebra.org).

Linear functions

A linear function is usually given by $f: x \rightarrow ax + b$, where $a, b \in \mathbb{Q}, x \in \mathbb{R}$.
To graph a linear function you need two points.

If the coefficient of the x part is positive ($a > 0$), the graph is **increasing**:	If the coefficient of the x part is zero ($a = 0$), the graph is **horizontal**:	If the coefficient of the x part is negative ($a < 0$), the graph is **decreasing**:
e.g. $y = 2x + 3$	e.g. $y = 3$	e.g. $y = -2x + 3$
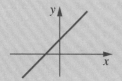	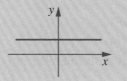	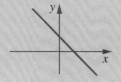

Graphing linear functions is covered extensively under the topic of Coordinate Geometry of the Line, which can be found in *Less Stress More Success Junior Cycle Maths Book 2*. There is also a connection between linear functions and arithmetic patterns.

{(2, 4), (3, 6), (4, 8), (5, 10)} are four couples of a function *f*.

(i) Plot the four couples.

(ii) The function *f* is derived by a rule. Suggest a rule for *f*.

(iii) On your diagram in **(i)**, plot and label two other couples which could be gotten from the same rule.

Solution

(i) Plotting the points given
   (plotted in blue on the graph):

The points form a straight line, so the line joining them would be a linear function.

Plotting points: (*x*, *y*)
= (horizontal, vertical)
= (over/back, up/down)
= (input, output)

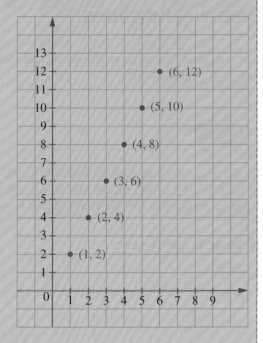

(ii) In the first couple, $x = 2$ and $y = 4$.
   In the second couple, $x = 3$ and $y = 6$.
   In the third couple, $x = 4$ and $y = 8$.

   Looking at the pattern we can see that the *y*-values are twice the *x*-values in each case. So the rule is $y = 2x$.

(iii) More couples which follow the rule $y = 2x$ are. (1, 2) or (6, 12).
   These points are marked in red on the diagram in **(i)**.

Part **(i)** was worth 15 marks, with 10 marks awarded for correctly plotting any **one** point.

Part **(ii)** was worth 5 marks, with 3 marks awarded for any correct step.

Part **(iii)** was worth 5 marks, with 3 marks awarded for plotting either of the two points.

Example

(i) Graph the function $y = 2x + 1$ in the domain $-2 \leq x \leq 3$.

(ii) Using your graph, find the value for y when $x = 2$.

Solution

(i) In order to graph a linear function, find the two points at the end of each line segment.

$$y = 2x + 1$$

If input, $x = -2$	If input, $x = 3$
Output, $y = 2(-2) + 1$	Output, $y = 2(3) + 1$
$y = -4 + 1$	$y = 6 + 1$
$y = -3$	$y = 7$
$(-2, -3)$	$(3, 7)$

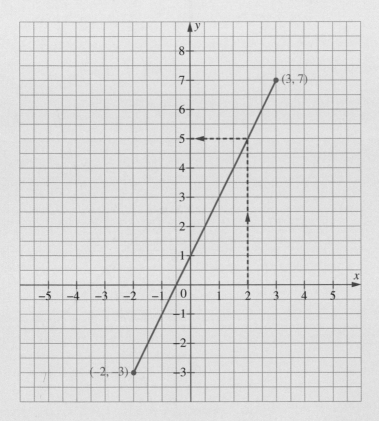

(ii) From the graph, when $x = 2$, $y = 5$ (the blue line on the graph).

Example

(i) On the same axes and scales, graph the functions $f: x \rightarrow 3x + 3$ and $g: x \rightarrow -x + 3$ in the domain $-2 \leq x \leq 2$.

(ii) From your graph, estimate the point where $f(x) = g(x)$ (the point where the two lines intersect).

Solution

(i) On the same axes and scales, graph the functions $f: x \rightarrow 3x + 3$ and $g: x \rightarrow -x + 3$ in the domain $-2 \leq x \leq 2$.

$$f(x) = 3x + 3$$

$x = -2$:	$x = 2$:
$f(x) = 3(-2) + 3$	$f(x) = 3(2) + 3$
$y = -6 + 3$	$y = 6 + 3$
$y = -3$	$y = 9$
$(-2, -3)$	$(2, 9)$

$$g(x) = -x + 3$$

$x = -2$:	$x = 2$:
$g(x) = -(-2) + 3$	$g(x) = -(2) + 3$
$y = 2 + 3$	$y = -2 + 3$
$y = 5$	$y = 1$
$(-2, 5)$	$(2, 1)$

Graphing the lines:

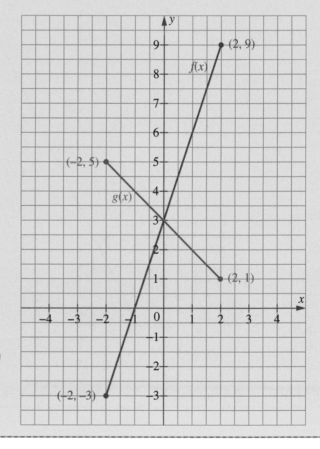

(ii) The lines intersect (cross) at the point $(0, 3)$.

Therefore, $f(x) = g(x)$ at the point $(0, 3)$.

A taxi has a base starting charge of €4. The passenger is then charged an additional €1·50 for every kilometre travelled.

(i) Write a function for the cost of a trip in terms of k where k is the number of kilometres travelled.

(ii) Graph the function in the domain from 0 km to 16 km.

(iii) Use your graph to find the cost of a trip which lasted 12 km.

(iv) Use your graph to find the distance covered during a trip which cost €13.

Solution

(i) Cost of a trip = Base charge of €4 + €1·50 per kilometre

$$c = €4 + €1·50(k)$$
$$c = 4 + 1·5(k)$$

(ii) Find the start and end points.

When $k = 0$ km:	When $k = 16$ km:
$c = 4 + 1·5(k)$	$c = 4 + 1·5(k)$
$c = 4 + 1·5(0)$	$c = 4 + 1·5(16)$
$c = 4 + 0$	$c = 4 + 24$
$c = 4$	$c = 28$
Start point: (0, 4)	End point: (0, 28)

Graph these points and join them to graph the function:

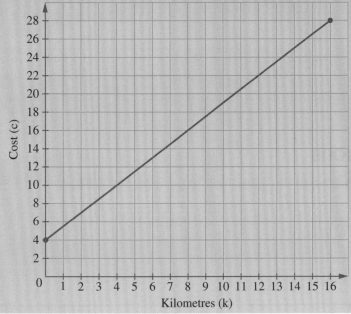

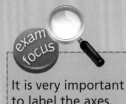

It is very important to label the axes. This makes the graph meaningful.

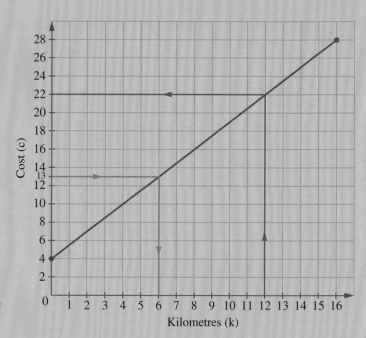

> **key point**
>
> A linear function can be represented by:
> $$y = \text{starting value} + (\text{rate of growth})x$$
> This is the same as a linear or arithmetic pattern.
> It is also the same as the equation of a line.
> $$y = mx + c$$
> Where m = rate of growth = slope
> $\qquad c$ = starting value = y-intercept
>
> (see booklet of formulae and tables)

(iii) From the graph (red line), when number of kilometres $k = 12$, the cost equals €22.

(iv) From the graph (green line), when the cost equals €13, the number of kilometres equals 6.

Quadratic functions

A quadratic function can be given in the form $f : x \rightarrow ax^2 + bx + c$, where $a \in \mathbb{N}, b, c \in \mathbb{Z}$, $x \in \mathbb{R}$ and $a \neq 0$.

Because of its shape, quite a few points are needed to accurately graph a quadratic function.

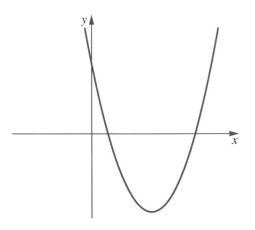

key point

The values where the graph of a quadratic function crosses the *x*-axis are known as the roots of the function. These are the values you get when you solve the quadratic equation formed, by letting the function equal zero.

Example

Draw a graph of the function $f : x \rightarrow x^2 + 3x - 1$ in the domain $-5 \leq x \leq 2$.

Solution

Complete a table.

x	$x^2 + 3x - 1$	y
−5	$(-5)^2 + 3(-5) - 1$	9
−4	$(-4)^2 + 3(-4) - 1$	3
−3	$(-3)^2 + 3(-3) - 1$	−1
−2	$(-2)^2 + 3(-2) - 1$	−3
−1	$(-1)^2 + 3(-1) - 1$	−3
0	$(0)^2 + 3(0) - 1$	−1
1	$(1)^2 + 3(1) - 1$	3
2	$(2)^2 + 3(2) - 1·$	9

The ordered pairs are
$(-5, 9), (-4, 3), (-3, -1), (-2, -3),$
$(-1, -3), (0, -1), (1, 3)$ and $(2, 9).$

Plot these points and join them up to graph the function $f(x)$.

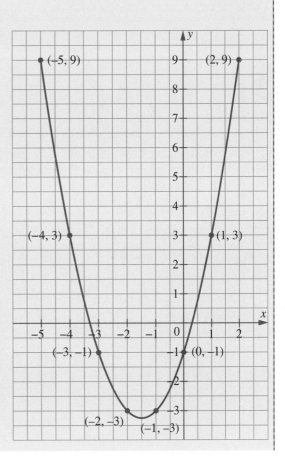

Alternative method to finding the points:

$f(-5) = (-5)^2 + 3(-5) - 1 = 9$ | $f(-1) = (-1)^2 + 3(-1) - 1 = -3$

$f(-4) = (-4)^2 + 3(-4) - 1 = 3$ | $f(0) = (0)^2 + 3(0) - 1 = -1$

$f(-3) = (-3)^2 + 3(-3) - 1 = -1$ | $f(1) = (1)^2 + 3(1) - 1 = 3$

$f(-2) = (-2)^2 + 3(-2) - 1 = -3$ | $f(2) = (2)^2 + 3(2) - 1 = 9$

The ordered pairs are $(-5, 9), (-4, 3), (-3, -1), (-2, -3), (-1, -3), (0, -1),$ $(1, 3)$ and $(2, 9)$.

exam focus

It is important that you show your workings when finding the outputs for the function. The 'Table' mode on the Casio calculator can be used to **check** these outputs. You can input the function and the domain of inputs and then the calculator will give all outputs. It's a good idea to practise this function on your calculator to become familiar with it.

exam Q

(i) Complete the following table for the function
$f: x \rightarrow x^2 - 3x - 2$ in the domain $-2 \le x \le 4, x \in \mathbb{R}$.

(ii) Using the values obtained in **(i)**, draw the graph of the function $f: x \rightarrow x^2 - 3x - 2$ in the domain $-2 \le x \le 4, x \in \mathbb{R}$.

Solution

(i) $f(x) = x^2 - 3x - 2$

$f(-2) = (-2)^2 - 3(-2) - 2 = 4 + 6 - 2 = 8$

$f(-1) = (-1)^2 - 3(-1) - 2 = 1 + 3 - 2 = 2$

$f(0) = (0)^2 - 3(0) - 2 = 0 + 0 - 2 = -2$

$f(1) = (1)^2 - 3(1) - 2 = 1 - 3 - 2 = -4$

$f(2) = (2)^2 - 3(2) - 2 = 4 - 6 - 2 = -4$

$f(3) = (3)^2 - 3(3) - 2 = 9 - 9 - 2 = -2$

$f(4) = (4)^2 - 3(4) - 2 = 16 - 12 - 2 = 2$

x	$f(x)$	$(x, f(x))$
-2	8	$(-2, 8)$
-1		
0		
1		
2		
3		
4		

(ii) Graph of the function:

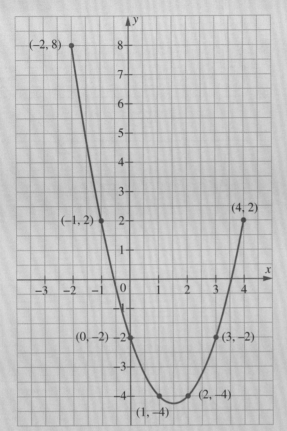

x	f(x)	(x, f(x))
−2	8	(−2, 8)
−1	2	(−1, 2)
0	−2	(0, −2)
1	−4	(1, −4)
2	−4	(2, −4)
3	−2	(3, −2)
4	2	(4, 2)

Part **(i)** was worth 15 marks, with 7 marks awarded for correctly evaluating any one correct value for $f(x)$ and 12 marks for evaluating four values of $f(x)$ correctly.

Part **(ii)** was worth 15 marks, with 7 marks awarded for correctly plotting any one point and 12 marks for correctly plotting any four points.

Make sure you attempt all parts. There are no marks for blanks!

Example

The graph shows the functions
$f(x) = x^2 - 9$ and $g(x) = x - 3$.
Use the graph to find the points
where $f(x) = g(x)$.

Solution

From the graph, we can see that the
functions cross, or intersect, at the
points $(-2, -5)$ and $(3, 0)$.

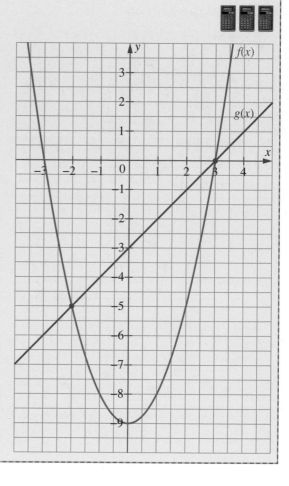

Exponential functions

On our course, an exponential function will be given in the form $f : x \to a2^x$ or
$f : x \to a3^x$, where $a \in \mathbb{N}$ and $x \in \mathbb{R}$.

key point

For exponential graphs in the
form $f(x) = a2^x$ or $f(x) = a3^x$:

The graph is increasing and the
curve intersects the y-axis at the
point $(0, a)$. This point is called
the focal point.

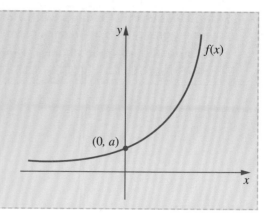

Example

The function, f, is defined as $f: x \rightarrow 5(3^x)$.

(i) Graph the function f in the domain $-2 \leq x \leq 2$.

(ii) Use the graph to estimate the value of x for which $f(x) = 30$.

Solution

(i)

x	$5(3^x)$	$f(x)$
-2	$5(3^{-2})$	$\dfrac{5}{9} = 0{\cdot}56$
-1	$5(3^{-1})$	$\dfrac{5}{3} = 1{\cdot}67$
0	$5(3^0)$	5
1	$5(3^1)$	15
2	$5(3^2)$	45

key point

Use the power button on your calculator to help you to work out the values of $f(x)$.

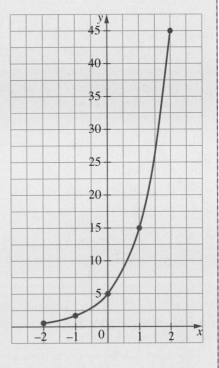

(ii) Go to 30 on the y-axis, go horizontally across to the graph and then drop a vertical line down to find the corresponding value of x.

When $f(x) = 30$, $x = 1{\cdot}6$.

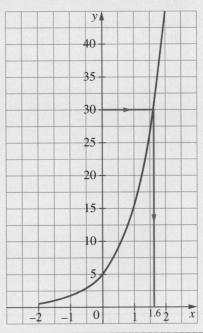

The number of bacteria, $B(t)$, in a sample after t hours can be represented by the model:

$$B(t) = 50(2^t).$$

(i) Graph the number of bacteria for the first 5 hours.

(ii) Use the graph to estimate the number of bacteria present after 4·5 hours.

(iii) Use to graph to estimate after how many hours there are 600 bacteria present in the sample.

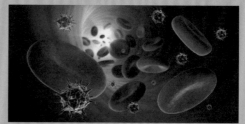

Solution

(i)

t	$50(2^t)$	$B(t)$
0	$50(2^0)$	50
1	$50(2^1)$	100
2	$50(2^2)$	200
3	$50(2^3)$	400
4	$50(2^4)$	800
5	$50(2^5)$	1 600

(ii) From the graph:
when $t = 4·5$ hours,
$B(4·5) = 1\ 120$
(red line).

(iii) From the graph:
when $B = 600$, $T = 3·6$ hours
(green line).

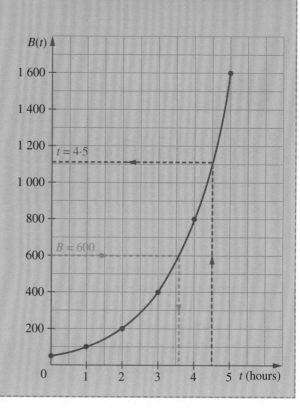

aims

☐ To be able to present numerical answers to the degree of accuracy specified

☐ To be able to make approximations and estimates of calculations

☐ To learn how to use ratio and proportion

☐ To draw and interpret graphs using direct proportion

Rounding

In the exam we are sometimes asked to round our answers.

The number 9·4837 = 9, correct to the nearest whole number

= 9·5, correct to one decimal place

= 9·48, correct to two decimal places

= 9·484, correct to three decimal places

The number 68 176 = 70 000, correct to one significant figure

= 68 000, correct to two significant figures

= 68 200, correct to three significant figures

key point

When expressing a whole number correct to a given number of significant figures, zeros at the end of the number are not counted, but must be included in the final result. All other zeros are significant, e.g. 90 426 = 90 400 correct to three significant figures.

exam Q

(i) Write the following numbers correct to the nearest ten.

121   195   504

(ii) Write the following numbers correct to three decimal places.

105·5555   2·173   0·0264

(iii) Write the following numbers correct to two significant figures.

2 920   159   0·0336

Solution

(i) 121 → 120

195 → 200

504 → 500

(ii) 105·5555 → 105·556

2·173 → 2·173

0·0264 → 0·026

(iii) 2 920 → 2 900

159 → 160

0·0336 → 0·034

Candidates had no idea how to answer this question. As a result, a **total** of 5 marks was awarded for all nine correct answers, with 3 marks awarded for any one correct answer! Remember, always write down **something**. This type of question may be asked again.

Changing units in the metric system

We are often required to change from one unit to another, as illustrated in the following exam question.

The booklet of formulae and tables may help.

(i) Change 5 000 g to kilograms.

(ii) Change 2·7 m to centimetres.

(iii) Change 8 000 cm³ to litres.

(iv) Change 4 m² to cm².

The booklet of formulae and tables gives us

$\text{Kilo} = 10^3 \ (= 1\ 000)$ and

$\text{Centi} = 10^{-2}\left(= \dfrac{1}{100}\right)$, that is,

$1 \text{ m} = 100 \text{ cm}$

Solution

(i) $5\ 000 \text{ g} = \dfrac{5\ 000}{1\ 000} = 5 \text{ kg}$

(ii) $2·7 \text{ m} = 2·7 \times 100 = 270 \text{ cm}$

(iii) $8\ 000 \text{ cm}^3 = \dfrac{8\ 000}{1\ 000} = 8 \ \ell$

(iv) $1 \text{ m} = 100 \text{ cm} \Rightarrow 1 \text{ m}^2 = 100 \times 100 \text{ cm}^2$

$4 \text{ m}^2 = 4 \times 100 \times 100 \text{ cm}^2 = 40\ 000 \text{ cm}^2$

$1 \ \ell = 1\ 000 \text{ cm}^3$

You must know this.

Each part above was worth 5 marks, with 3 marks awarded in each part for any one correct piece of work. Keep writing.

Estimates

There are many occasions when it is either desirable or necessary to round off large or small numbers to a reasonable degree of accuracy. With the widespread use of calculators, it is important that we have some estimate of the answer we expect to get. Then we will know whether the answer shown on the calculator is reasonable or not.

Jack had to estimate the cost of 396 teddy bears. The calculation he used was $396 \times 27 \cdot 25$.

Without a calculator, Jack has to estimate the answer.

396 is approximately 400.
27·25 is approximately 27.

Hence, an approximate answer is $400 \times 27 = €10\,800$.

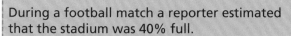

Croke Park in Dublin holds 82 300 people when full.

During a football match a reporter estimated that the stadium was 40% full.

How many people were estimated to be at the game?

Give your answer correct to the nearest 100 people.

Solution
100% = 82 300

$1\% = \dfrac{82\,300}{100} = 823$

40% = 823 × 40 = 32 920

To the nearest 100 people = 32 900.

Alternatively,

40% of the stadium = 82 300 × 0·40 = 32 920

Then to the nearest 100 people we write 32 900.

key
point

$40\% = \dfrac{40}{100} = \dfrac{4}{10} = 0 \cdot 4$

exam Q

(i) Karen went to a shop to buy five magazines. She had €10 to spend. She made an estimate of the total cost by correcting the price of each magazine to the next highest euro. The magazines cost €1·95, €1·99, €3·59, €1·40 and 99 cent. Work out her estimate.

(ii) Based on the estimate, would she think she had enough money?

(iii) Work out the exact cost of the magazines.

(iv) Suggest what you think is a better method for estimating the total cost of the magazines. Give a reason for your answer.

Solution

(i) €1·95 → 2·00

€1·99 → 2·00

€3·59 → 4·00

€1·40 → 2·00

€0·99 → 1·00

Total = €11·00

(ii) Since her estimate is €11 and she has €10 to spend, she concludes that she does not have enough money.

exam focus

If Karen's answer to part **(i)** was €10 or less, she would in part **(ii)** conclude that she had enough money.

This type of question, which has two opposite and contradictory answers where both are awarded full marks, often appears on the exam. **Always** write down your opinion and back it up with your work clearly shown. This will maximise your final result.

(iii) 1·95 + 1·99 + 3·59 + 1·40 + 0·99 = €9·92

(iv) It would be more accurate if Karen rounded to the nearest whole number.

This is likely to give a better estimate, as some prices will round up and some will round down.

exam focus

The above question was worth a total of 25 marks.

It was not well answered.

However, part **(iii)** was easy and well answered. It was awarded 10 marks. Even if you cannot do the first part of a question, you should continue on and attempt all parts.

Eight people ate at a restaurant. Each meal was approximately the same cost. The bill was €128. A service charge of 10% was then added.

Michelle said, '€15 each is enough to pay the bill and service charge'.

(i) Do you agree with her estimate?   Yes ☐ No ☐
Give a reason for your answer.

(ii) Can you suggest a better estimate? Give a reason for your answer.

This question was awarded a total of 15 marks. The easy part **(i)** was awarded 10 of those marks. Be sure to answer each part of each question to the best of your ability and you will do very well.

Solution

(i) €15 each from 8 people = €120.

This is not enough to pay the bill of €128.

We do not agree with Michelle's estimate. No ☑

10% of €128 = €12·80

(ii) The total bill = 128 + 12·80 = €140·80

Shared equally by 8 people means €140·80 ÷ 8 = €17·60.

Hence, any amount greater than or equal to €17·60 is a better estimate. The calculations above are my reason.

Ratio and proportion

Ratios are used to compare quantities. We can be asked to divide quantities in a given ratio and solve problems on proportion.

€400 is shared between Mary and Tom in the ratio 7:3. How much does each receive?

Solution

7 + 3 = 10 parts

So: 1 part = $\dfrac{€400}{10}$ = €40

7 parts = 40 × 7 = €280 for Mary

3 parts = 40 × 3 = €120 for Tom

A sum of money was divided in the ratio 3:2. The larger amount was €39. What was the total amount of money?

Solution

This question gives us an equation in disguise.

3 parts = €39

1 part = $\dfrac{39}{3}$ = €13

Then 3 parts + 2 parts = 5 parts = Total amount

Hence, 5 parts = 13 × 5 = €65 is the total amount of money.

Example

€5 580 is shared between Fred and Ciara in the ratio of their ages. Fred is three times as old as Ciara.

(i) Write down the ratio of their ages.

(ii) How much money does each receive?

(iii) How much money would Fred have to give to Ciara so that they would have equal amounts?

Solution

(i) Fred:Ciara = 3:1

(ii) 3 + 1 = 4 is the total number of parts.

1 part = $\dfrac{5\,580}{4}$ = €1 395,   hence, 3 parts = 1 395 × 3 = €4 185

Ciara gets €1 395 and Fred gets €4 185.

(iii)

For both to have equal parts, the calculation is $\dfrac{5\,580}{2}$ = €2 790.

Hence, for Fred and Ciara to have equal amounts, Fred must give Ciara 4 185 − 2 790 = €1 395.

Directly proportional graphs

If a graph of two variables is a straight line through the origin, then one variable is **directly proportional** to the other. This means that if one variable changes, then the other also changes by the same ratio.

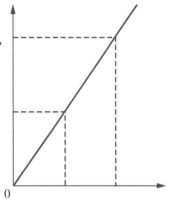

Example

Noah is filling this cylinder with water.
The water is being delivered from the tap
at the rate of 120 ml/sec.
Noah times how long it takes to
fill the cylinder.

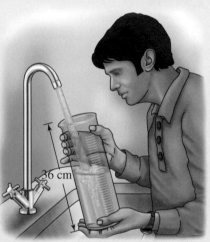

Height of water (cm)	6	12	18	24	30	36
Time taken (sec)	1·2	2·4	3·6	4·8	6·0	7·2

(i) Draw a graph of height against time.

(ii) Use your graph to find the height of the
water after 5 seconds.

(iii) How long does it take for the water to reach a height of 20 cm?

Solution

(i)

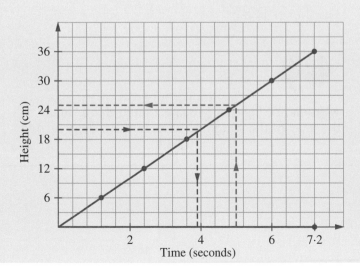

(ii) From the graph after 5 seconds the height is 25 cm.

(iii) From the graph a height of 20 cm is reached after 3·9 seconds.

The rate of flow of 120 ml/sec is not required in our solution.

Example

The previous question based on Noah filling the cylinder with water may be presented in the following way:

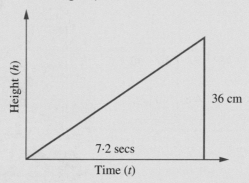

Height (h)

36 cm

7·2 secs

Time (t)

Use the gradient of the graph to find the rule connecting the two variables.

Solution

The gradient = The slope = m = $\dfrac{\text{Rise}}{\text{Run}} = \dfrac{36}{7\cdot2} = \dfrac{360}{72} = 5$

A gradient (slope) of 5 means that in this example, the level of the water increases by 5 cm every second.

In which of these graphs is q directly proportional to t?

(i)

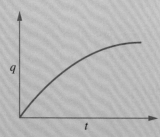

(ii)

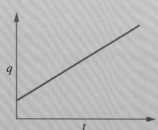

(iii)

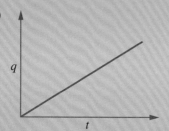

(iv)

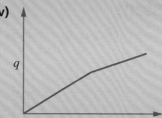

Solution

(i) Is not a straight line, hence not directly proportional.

(ii) Does not pass through the origin, hence not directly proportional.

(iii) A straight line through the origin indicates t and q are directly proportional.

(iv) Is not a complete straight line, hence not directly proportional.

15 Distance, Speed, Time and Graphs of Motion

Metric system

It is important to be able to convert units in the metric system.

exam Q

A swimming pool is 50 m in length. Mary swims 25 lengths of the pool. What distance does Mary swim

(i) in metres   **(ii)** in kilometres?

Solution

(i) 50 m × 25 lengths = 1 250 m

key point

$$1\ 000\ m = 1\ km$$

(ii) $1\ 250\ m = \dfrac{1\ 250}{1\ 000}\ km = 1 \cdot 25\ km$

Converting minutes to hours

To convert minutes to hours, **divide by** 60.

For example, 36 minutes $= \dfrac{36}{60} = \dfrac{6}{10} = \dfrac{3}{5} = 0 \cdot 6$ hours.

The following occur often and are easy to memorise

15 minutes $= \dfrac{1}{4}$ hour;   20 minutes $= \dfrac{1}{3}$ hour;   10 minutes $= \dfrac{1}{6}$ hour.

Converting hours to minutes

To convert fractions, or decimals, of an hour to minutes, **multiply by** 60.

For example; $\dfrac{2}{3}$ hour $= \dfrac{2}{3} \times 60 = \dfrac{120}{3} = 40$ minutes.

$0 \cdot 75$ hour $= 0 \cdot 75 \times 60 = 45$ minutes

Distance, speed and time

There are three formulas to remember when dealing with problems involving distance (D), speed (S) and time (T). **Note:** Speed here means average speed.

1. Speed $= \dfrac{\text{Distance}}{\text{Time}}$ **2.** Time $= \dfrac{\text{Distance}}{\text{Speed}}$ **3.** Distance $=$ Speed $\times$ Time

It can be difficult to remember these formulae. To help you remember, consider the triangle on the right. By covering the quantity required (*D, S* or *T*), any of the three formulas above can be found by inspection.

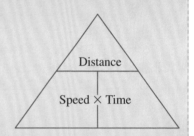

Common units of speed

1. Kilometres per hour, written as km/h.
2. Metres per second, written as m/s.

Marks may be lost if you do not include units in your answers, where appropriate.

Cormac went by car from Limerick to Cork, a journey of 100 km. He travelled at an average speed of 80 km/h.

(i) How many hours and minutes did it take Cormac to complete the journey?

(ii) Cormac left Limerick at 11:15. At what time did he arrive in Cork?

(iii) Cormac's car used 1 litre of petrol for every 16 km travelled. On that day, petrol cost 155 cent per litre. Find the cost of the petrol used on Cormac's journey from Limerick to Cork. Give your answer to the nearest euro.

Solution

(i) Time = $\dfrac{\text{Distance}}{\text{Speed}} = \dfrac{100}{80} = 1.25$ hours

$= 1.25$ hours $= 1\frac{1}{4}$ hours $=$ 1 hour and 15 minutes

(ii) 11:15   Left Limerick
     + 1:15
     12:30   Arrives in Cork

(iii) Number of litres required $= \dfrac{\text{Distance travelled}}{16}$

$= \dfrac{100}{16}$

$= 6.25$ litres

Cost $= 6.25 \times 155$ cents $= 968.75$ cents $= €9.6875$

Answer: petrol costs €10 to the nearest euro.

The following is part of a bus timetable from Galway to Limerick.

		Time		
Galway	depart	06:40	07:20	07:50
Oranmore	depart	06:48	07:28	07:57
Gort	depart	07:36	08:16	08:45
Ennis	depart	08:05	08:45	09:14
Limerick	depart	08:45	09:25	09:44

(a) James lives in Oranmore. He needs to be in Limerick by 09:30.

  (i) What is the latest time that James can get the bus from Oranmore?

  (ii) How long does his bus journey take, from Oranmore to Limerick?

(b) It takes Gina 1 hour and 15 minutes to drive from Oranmore to Limerick.

  (i) What fraction of an hour is 15 minutes?

  (ii) The distance from Oranmore to Limerick is 90 km. Work out Gina's average speed for the journey, in km/hour.

Solution

(a) (i) To arrive in Limerick by 09:30, James needs to catch the bus at 07:28 from Oranmore.

(ii) Length of bus journey:

$$09:25 \Rightarrow 08:85$$
$$-\ 07:28 \qquad -\ 07:28$$
$$\overline{\qquad\qquad} \qquad \overline{1:57}$$

Transfer one hour into the minutes column.

Therefore, the bus journey is 1 hour 58 minutes

(b) (i) To convert minutes into hours, divide by 60: $\dfrac{15}{60} = \dfrac{1}{4}$ of an hour

(ii) Speed $= \dfrac{\text{Distance}}{\text{Time}} = \dfrac{90}{1 \cdot 25} = 72$ km/hr

Peter travelled 50 km to a football match and he returned home by the same route when the match was over.

(i) Peter travelled to the match at an average speed of 60 km/h. How many minutes did the journey to the match take?

(ii) Peter arrived at the match at 17:35. At what time did he leave from home to travel to the match?

(iii) Peter took 75 minutes to travel home from the match. Calculate the average speed, in km/h, for this journey.

Solution

(i) Time $= \dfrac{\text{Distance}}{\text{Speed}} = \dfrac{50}{60} = \dfrac{5}{6}$ hours

Time $= \dfrac{5}{6} \times 60$ minutes

Time $= 50$ minutes

(ii) Arrived at 17:35

Travel time 50 minutes

Transfer one hour into the minutes column.

$$17:35 \Rightarrow 16:95$$
$$-\ \ \ 50 \qquad\quad -\ \ \ 50$$
$$\overline{\qquad\quad} \qquad \overline{16:45}$$

This is the time Peter left home

(iii) 75 minutes to travel 50 km

1 minute to travel $\dfrac{50}{75}$ km

60 minutes to travel $\dfrac{50 \times 60}{75}$ km

$\dfrac{50 \times 60}{75} = 40$ by calculator.

The average speed for this journey is 40 km/hour.

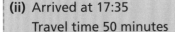

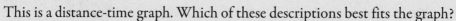

Example

This is a distance-time graph. Which of these descriptions best fits the graph?

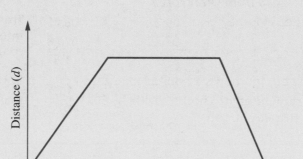

(i) Bert walks to Ernie's house, stays a while and then returns home.

or

(ii) Bert walks up a hill, along a flat path, and then walks down a second hill.

Solution

(i) The answer is **(i)** because: we can say Bert travels from Ernie's house at a faster speed than he went to Ernie's house because the line on the graph is steeper in the third section.

The steepness of the lines on the above graph indicate speed. The steeper the line, the greater the speed. Also the line is flat for a while, indicating the distance did not change.

Olive cycled to the shop to get some milk for her tea. She cycled along a particular route and returned by the same route. The graph below shows the different stages of her journey.

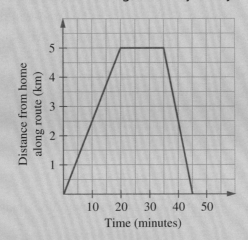

(i) How long did Olive stay in the shop?

(ii) How far from her home is the shop?

(iii) Compare the speed of her trip to the shop with her speed on the way home.

(iv) Write a paragraph to describe her journey.

Solution (i) and (ii)

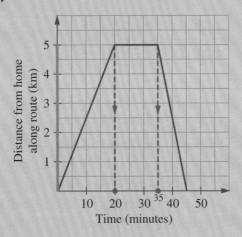

Reading from the graph, Olive stayed in the shop for 35 − 20 = 15 minutes.

Reading from the graph, Olive's home is 5 km, or 5 000 m, from the shop.

(iii) Speed to the shop

$$= \frac{\text{Distance}}{\text{Time}}$$

$$= \frac{5\,000}{20}$$

$$= 250 \text{ m per minute}$$

Speed to her home

$$= \frac{\text{Distance}}{\text{Time}}$$

$$= \frac{5\,000}{10}$$

$$= 500 \text{ m per minute}$$

Comparing the two speeds we conclude Olive travelled home at twice the speed.

(iv) Olive cycled for 20 minutes at a speed of 250 m per minute on her way to the shop. She spent 15 minutes at the shop. On her return journey she cycled twice as fast and got home in 10 minutes.

The graph below shows some details about a journey Alex made by bicycle.

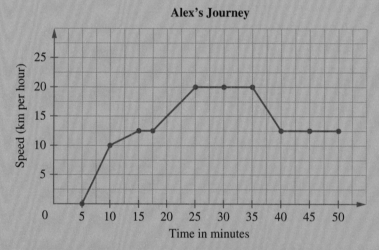

Alex's Journey

Alex waited for his friend before he set off on his journey.

(i) How long did he wait before setting out?

(ii) What was Alex's highest speed during the journey?

(iii) For what length of time was Alex travelling at the highest speed?

(iv) How far did Alex travel at the highest speed?

Solution

(i) Alex waited 5 minutes before setting out.

(ii) Alex had a highest speed of 20 km per hour.

Candidates lost 1 mark if the unit (minutes) was omitted.

(iii)

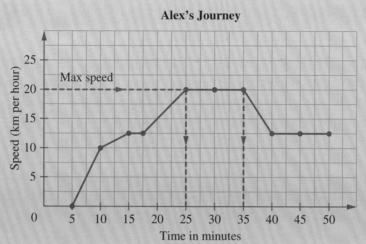

Alex's Journey

Alex travelled at maximum speed from 25 minutes to 35 minutes, that is, for 10 minutes he travelled at maximum speed.

Candidates with answers close to the above answers were awarded full marks, e.g. for part **(iii)** 8 minutes was accepted, 11 minutes was accepted.

(iv) He travels at a speed of 20 km per hour for 10 minutes.

Distance = Speed × Time

$$= 20 \times \frac{10}{60}$$

$$= \frac{200}{60}$$

$$= \frac{10}{3} \text{ km}$$

We write the time in hours.

This question was awarded a total of 25 marks, as follows:

  (i) 10 marks

 (ii) 5 marks

(iii) 5 marks

(iv) 5 marks

It is worth noting that the highest mark was given for the easiest question. Remember to write down **something** in each of the spaces provided for answers on the exam paper.

Example

Match each explanation to the correct graph.

(i) Rebecca walks part of the way to the shop and runs the rest of the way. She completes her shopping and runs all the way back home.

(ii) Bren walks to the shop and does some shopping. On the way home, being tired, Bren stops for a rest. He then walks very slowly the rest of the way home.

(iii) Noah goes for a walk to the post-box, posts his letter and returns home. He walks at a constant speed in both directions.

(iv) Elaine walked to Carol's house and stayed for tea. After tea Carol gave her a lift home in her car.

P

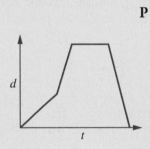

Q

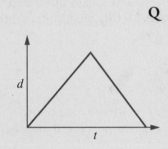

R

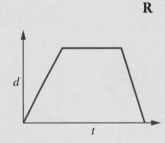

S

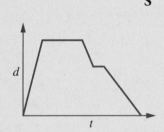

Solution

Rebecca walks part of the way to the shop and runs the rest of the way. She completes her shopping and runs all the way back home.

Explanation (i) matches graph P.

Notice that the flat section represents the time Rebecca spends in the shop.

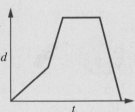

Bren walks to the shop and does some shopping. On the way home, being tired, Bren stops for a rest. He then walks very slowly the rest of the way home.
Explanation (ii) matches graph S.

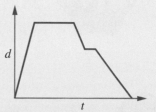

Notice that the two flat sections represent when Bren visits the shop and when he stops for a rest.

Noah goes for a walk to the post-box, posts his letter and returns home. He walks at a constant speed in both directions.
Explanation (iii) matches graph Q.
Notice that as Noah does not stop on his journey, there are no flat sections.

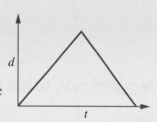

Elaine walks to Carol's house and stays for tea. After tea Carol gives her a lift home in her car.
Explanation (iv) matches graph R.
Notice that the line representing Elaine's journey home by car is much **steeper** than the line representing her walk to Carol's house. This is because she travels much **faster** by car.

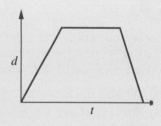

16 Arithmetic and Financial Maths

aims

☐ To handle calculations involving money
☐ To learn how to calculate household bills and VAT
☐ To learn how to convert currencies or foreign exchange
☐ To learn how to calculate percentage profit or loss
☐ To learn how to calculate compound interest
☐ To learn how to calculate income tax and take-home pay

Calculations with money

exam Q

Kathy and Jack Byrne have four children. A family ticket for the cinema costs €19·50. A family ticket is for two adults and two children. A single adult ticket costs €7·25 and a single child ticket costs €4·50.

(i) What is the total cost of a family ticket and two child tickets?

(ii) If an individual ticket was bought for each member of the family, what would be the extra cost?

Solution

(i) A family ticket costs €19·50.

Two child tickets cost €4·50 × 2 = €9·00.

Total cost of a family ticket and two child tickets

= 19·50 + 9·00

= €28·50

(ii) Two adult tickets cost €7·25 × 2 = €14·50.

Four child tickets cost €4·50 × 4 = €18·00.

Total cost = €32·50.

The extra cost is given by

€32·50 − €28·50 = €4·00.

exam focus

This question was awarded a total of 15 marks: 10 marks for part **(i)** and 5 marks for part **(ii)**. Take good care doing the calculations and full marks can be gained quickly and efficiently.

Pat is a waiter at a restaurant. He is paid €8·65 per hour. He can also get tips. Last week he worked for 22 hours. Pat's wages plus tips were €235·50 in total for the week.

How much did Pat make on tips last week?

Solution

Wages found by €8·64 × 22 hours = €190·08.

The tips are found by €235·50 − €190·08 = €45·42 in tips.

This question was awarded a total of 15 marks, with a minimum award of 7 marks for any one correct step. However, full marks must be your goal here.

Lisa is saving to buy a laptop. It costs €320. Each week she saves the same amount of money. She has €50 saved to begin with.

After 18 weeks, Lisa will have exactly enough money saved to buy the laptop.

Work out how much money Lisa saves each week.

Solution

Amount to be saved = €320 − €50

Amount to be saved = €270

Amount to save per week = $\dfrac{€270}{18}$ = €15

Example

The price of a holiday is increased by 8% to €1 782. What was the original cost of the holiday?

Solution

$$100\% = \boxed{\begin{array}{c} \text{Original} \\ \text{cost of holiday} \end{array}} \xrightarrow{+8\%} \boxed{€1\ 782} = 108\%$$

$$\text{We write} \quad 108\% = €1\ 782$$

$$1\% = \frac{1\ 782}{108}$$

$$100\% = \frac{1\ 782}{108} \times 100 = €1\ 650$$

Therefore, the original cost of the holiday was €1 650.

Household bills and VAT

Value-added tax, or VAT, is a government tax which is added to many of the things that we buy. VAT is usually expressed as a percentage. When dealing with problems involving percentages, it is very important to be able to convert a percentage to a decimal. A calculator is particularly useful in these situations.

key point

To find 25%, multiply by $0.25 = \dfrac{25}{100} = \dfrac{1}{4}$

To find 110%, multiply by $1.10 = \dfrac{110}{100} = \dfrac{11}{10}$

To find 13.5%, multiply by $0.135 = \dfrac{135}{1\ 000} = \dfrac{27}{200}$

Jack takes his car to a garage for a service and receives an itemised bill. Find the total cost of servicing the car.

Itemised bill for service	Cost
5 litres of oil at €4·20 per litre	
2 windscreen wiper blades at €4·50 per blade	
2 brake shoes at €28 each	
2 hours of labour at €60 per hour	
Subtotal (before VAT added)	
VAT @ 13·5%	
Total bill	

Solution

€4·20 × 5 = €21·00 for oil

€4·50 × 2 = €9·00 for wiper blades

€28 × 2 = €56·00 for brake shoes

€60 × 2 = €120 for labour

€206·00 subtotal

To calculate the VAT:

$$100\% = €206$$

$$1\% = \frac{206}{100} \quad \text{(divide both sides by 100)}$$

$$\text{VAT} = 13\cdot5\% = \frac{206}{100} \times 13\cdot5 \quad \text{(multiply both sides by 13.5)}$$

$$\text{VAT} = 13\cdot5\% = €27\cdot81$$

Total bill = 206·00 + 27·81 = €233·81

Example

A telephone bill, including VAT at 23%, came to €116·85. Calculate the bill without VAT.

Solution

$$100\% = \boxed{\begin{array}{c}\text{Bill before VAT}\\\text{is added on}\end{array}} \xrightarrow{+23\%} \boxed{€116·85} = 123\%$$

We then write

$$123\% = €116·85$$

$$1\% = \frac{116·85}{123} \qquad \text{(divide both sides by 123)}$$

$$100\% = \frac{116·85 \times 100}{123} \qquad \text{(multiply both sides by 100)}$$

The bill without VAT = 100% = €95·00.

Alex's gas bill gave the following data:

Unit type	Present reading	Previous reading	Unit price
Day rate	42 384	40 932	€0·1702
Night rate	16 528	15 791	€0·0951

(i) Calculate the total cost of the units used, to the nearest cent.

(ii) Alex also pays a standing charge of €28·12 and a levy of €6·38. VAT is charged on all amounts. If the total amount of Alex's gas bill is €429·10, find the amount of VAT.

Solution

(i) Number of units used = Present reading – Previous reading

<table>
<tr><td colspan="2" align="center">Day rate</td><td colspan="2" align="center">Night rate</td></tr>
</table>

Day rate		Night rate	
Present reading:	42 384	Present reading:	16 528
Previous reading:	40 932	Previous reading:	15 791
	1 452 units		737 units
	× €0·1702		× €0·0951
Cost:	€247·1304	Cost:	€70·0887

Total cost of units: €247·1304 + €70·0887 = €317·2191 = €317·22

(ii) Charges:

Units:　€317·22
Standing charge:　€28·12
Levy:　€6·38
Total of charges:　€351·72

Total of bill = Total of charges + VAT

€429·10 = €351·72 + VAT

€77·38 = VAT

Currency exchange

If we travel to a country not in the eurozone, we generally change our euro, €, to the currency of that country.

If you see €1 = 125 yen, ¥, displayed in a bank, how do you convert ¥10 000 to €?

We write ¥125 = €1

$$¥1 = €\frac{1}{125}$$

$$¥10\,000 = €\frac{1}{125} \times 10\,000 = €80$$

key point

Put the currency required on the right-hand side of the equation.

Example

On a certain day, €1 = $1·42.

(i) How many dollars would you get for €750?

(ii) How many euros would you get for $9 585?

Solution

(i)　€1 = $1·42　　　　　(dollars on the right, because we want our answer in dollars)

€750 = $1·42 × 750　　(multiply both sides by 750)

€750 = $1 065

(ii)　$1·42 = €1　　　　(euros on the right, because we want our answer in euros)

$$\$1 = €\frac{1}{1·42}$$　　　　(divide both sides by 1·42)

$$\$9\,585 = €\frac{1}{1·42} \times 9\,585$$　　(multiply both sides by 9 585)

$9,585 = €6 750

A hotel website gives the cost of staying for three nights in a hotel in Copenhagen as 2 925 Danish kroner.

(i) Find the cost in euro, given that €1 = 7·5 Danish kroner.

(ii) This cost includes a 5% service charge for the website company. Find, in euro, how much the hotel will get for the three-night stay. Give your answer to two decimal places.

Solution

(i) 7·5 Danish kroner = €1

1 Danish kroner = €$\dfrac{1}{7·5}$

2,925 Danish kroner = €$\dfrac{1}{7·5}$ × 2 925 = €390

(ii) The cost of €390 includes a 5% service charge.

105% = €390

1% = €3·714285

100% = €371·4285

Therefore, the hotel will receive €371·43.

Amina wants to buy a pair of runners.

(a) She can buy them online for £51·24. The currency conversion rate is €1 = £0·90. Convert £51·24 to euro. Give your answer correct to the nearest cent.

(b) The same runners are for sale in a local sports shop for €65. Amina has a voucher for 15% off anything she buys in this shop. Work out how much the runners will cost Amina if she uses this voucher.

Solution

(a) £0·90 = €1

£1 = €$\dfrac{1}{(0·9)}$

£51·24 = €$\dfrac{1}{(0·9)}$ × 51·24

£51·24 = €56·93

(b) % of €65 = €9·75

Discounted price: €6155 − €9·75

= €55·25

Percentage profit and loss and selling price

Profit and loss are often given as a percentage of the cost price. This is useful when we need to compare profit or loss on different items. Percentage profit or loss is calculated with the following formulae:

$$\text{Percentage profit} = \frac{\text{Profit}}{\text{Cost price}} \times 100\%$$

$$\text{Percentage loss} = \frac{\text{Loss}}{\text{Cost price}} \times 100\%$$

Example

Compact discs are bought for €10 each and sold for €15·50 each. Find the profit made on 20 compact discs.

Solution

Profit per disc = €15·50 − €10 = €5·50.
Profit made on 20 discs = €5·50 × 20 = €110.

key point

Profit = Sell price − Buy price

Example

Rebecca bought a car for €15 880 and sold it for €19 850.
Calculate her profit as a percentage of
  (i) the cost price
  (ii) the selling price

Solution

Profit = 19 850 − 15 880 = €3 970

(i) Profit as a percentage of cost price

$$= \frac{\text{Profit}}{\text{Cost price}} \times 100$$

$$= \frac{3\,970}{15\,880} \times 100$$

$$= 25\%$$

(ii) Profit as a percentage of selling price

$$= \frac{\text{Profit}}{\text{Selling price}} \times 100$$

$$= \frac{3\,970}{19\,850} \times 100$$

$$= 20\%$$

An exam question may ask you to explain or comment on why profit as a percentage of cost price and selling price are not equal. The answer is because one is over cost price while the other is over selling price. The above example shows why this is so.

Discounts

A discount is a reduction in the selling price. A discount is typically given to encourage customers to buy a product or to pay for a product in advance or in cash.

$$\text{Percentage discount} = \frac{\text{Discount}}{\text{Selling price}} \times 100\%$$

Example

A shop sold a TV for €1 071. This included a 16% discount. Calculate the price of the TV before the discount was allowed.

Solution

$100\% = $ | Original cost of TV | $\xrightarrow{-16\%}$ | €1 071 | $= 84\%$

We write $\quad 84\% = €1\,071$

$$1\% = \frac{1\,071}{84}$$

$$100\% = \frac{1\,071}{84} \times 100 = €1\,275$$

$100\% - 16\% = 84\%$

Hence, the original cost of the TV was €1 275.

Example

The price of a laptop is €700. In a sale the price of this laptop is reduced to €595. What is the percentage reduction on the original price of the laptop?

Solution

The selling price is the original price and **not** the sale price. Watch out for this.

Discount = 700 − 595 = €105

$$\text{Percentage discount} = \frac{\text{Discount}}{\text{Selling price}} \times 100\%$$

$$= \frac{105}{700} \times 100\% = 15\%$$

Interest

Interest is the sum of money that you pay for borrowing money or that is paid to you for lending money.

Example

€6 400 was invested for one year and amounted to €6 624 at the end of that year. Calculate the rate of interest per annum.

Solution

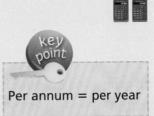

Per annum = per year

Interest = €6 624 − €6 400 = €224

$$\text{Rate of interest} = \frac{\text{Interest}}{\text{Sum invested}} \times 100\% = \frac{224 \times 100\%}{6\,400} = 3 \cdot 5\%$$

A sum of money invested at 10% per annum interest amounts to €907·50 after one year. How much was invested?

Solution

$$100\% = \boxed{\begin{array}{c}\text{Amount}\\\text{invested}\end{array}} \xrightarrow{+10\%} \boxed{\text{€}907\text{·}50} = 110\%$$

We then write
$$110\% = \text{€}907\text{·}50$$

$$1\% = \frac{907\text{·}50}{110} \qquad \text{(divide both sides by 110)}$$

$$100\% = \frac{907\text{·}50}{110} \times 100 \qquad \text{(multiply both sides by 100)}$$

The amount invested $= 100\% = \text{€}825.$

Compound interest

The formula for calculating compound interest is given in the booklet of formulae and tables.

$F = P(1 + i)^t$, where F = final value (amount)

$\qquad\qquad P$ = principal

$\qquad\qquad i$ = interest rate

$\qquad\qquad t$ = number of years

i is always given in decimal form.

$i = 5\% = 0\text{·}05$

$i = 16\% = 0\text{·}16$

$i = 3\text{·}5\% = 0\text{·}035$, etc.

Final amount is principal + interest.

With compound interest, the interest earned each year is added to the principal to form a new principal. This new principal earns interest in the next year and so on.

The examination questions will not require you to calculate compound interest beyond **three** years. The formula is very efficient when combined with a calculator. However, the formula does **not** work if:

(i) The interest rate, i, is changed during the time period or

(ii) Money is added or subtracted during the time period.

Example

Calculate the compound interest on €8 800 for three years at 5% per annum.

> **key point**
>
> In this question we use the formula because the interest rate does not change, nor is any money added or subtracted.

Solution

Given $P = 8\,800$, $i = 5\% = 0{\cdot}05$ and $t = 3$

$$F = P(1 + i)^t$$
$$F = 8\,800\,(1 + 0{\cdot}05)^3$$
$$F = 10\,187{\cdot}1 \qquad \text{(using a calculator)}$$

Compound interest $= F - P = 10\,187{\cdot}1 - 8\,800 = €1\,387{\cdot}10$

Walter borrows €5 000 for two years at 7% per annum compound interest. He repays €2 000 at the end of the first year.

How much must he repay at the end of the second year to clear his loan?

Solution

Principal for first year = 100% = €5 000

$$1\% = \frac{5\,000}{100}$$

$$7\% = \frac{5\,000}{100} \times 7 = €350$$

> **key point**
>
> We cannot use the formula in this case.

At the end of the first year, Walter owes 5 000 + 350 = €5 350.

He then repays €2 000, which means the principal for the second year is €5 350 − €2 000 = €3 350.

Principal for the second year = 100% = €3 350

$$1\% = \frac{3\,350}{100}$$

$$7\% = \frac{3\,350}{100} \times 7 = €234{\cdot}5$$

At the end of the second year Walter owes €3 350 + €234·5 = €3 584·50.

To clear his loan he must repay €3 584·50.

Income tax

The following two equations are very important when calculating income tax.

> Gross tax − Tax credits = Tax payable
>
> Net income = Gross income − Tax paid

Net income is also called take-home pay.

Carla's gross pay is €24 000. Her tax credit is €2 500. She pays income tax at the rate of 22%. What is her take-home pay?

Gross Pay	€24 000
Tax @ 22%	
Tax Credit	€2 500
Tax Due	
Take-home Pay	

Solution

$$100\% = 24\ 000$$

$$1\% = \frac{24\ 000}{100}$$

$$\text{Tax @22\%} = \frac{24\ 000 \times 22}{100} = 5\ 280 \qquad \text{(by calculator)}$$

Tax due = Tax payable − Tax credit

$$= 5\ 280 - 2\ 500$$

$$= 2\ 780$$

Take-home pay = Gross pay − Tax due

$$= 24\ 000 - 2\ 780$$

$$= €21\ 220$$

Answer

Gross Pay	€24 000
Tax @ 22%	5 280
Tax Credit	€2 500
Tax Due	2 780
Take-home Pay	21 220

The table below shows the three graphs A, B, and C. Each graph shows the tax that someone must pay depending on their gross income. Each graph begins at (0, 0)

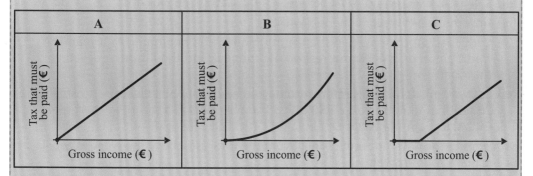

Jean's tax rate is 20% of her gross income. She has a tax credit of €3 000. Which graph shows the tax that Jean must pay depending on her gross income, taking her tax credit into account?
Justify your answer.

Solution

Answer: Graph C

Justification: Jean has a tax credit of €3 000 which means that she won't pay tax at all if her gross income is below a certain amount (€15 000 in this question, since 20% of €15 000 is €3 000).

Graph C is the only graph where tax initially stays at zero while gross income increases. Once her income exceeds €15 000, she will start paying tax and so the graph rises.

(i) Cathy works in a bakery and earns €8·65 per hour. She works 40 hours a week. Find Cathy's gross pay for the week.

(ii) Cathy has to pay income tax at a rate of 20%. Find Cathy's gross tax.

(iii) She has a tax credit of €20 per week. Find Cathy's net tax.

(iv) How much per week is she left with?

(v) Cathy had €1 650 saved in the credit union at the beginning of a year. The credit union paid 4·5% interest on her money. Find the interest earned in that year.

(vi) Cathy wants to use this interest to pay an electricity bill. Electricity costs 20 cent per unit. She used 250 units. The bill also has a standing charge of €30. Calculate the electricity bill.

(vii) Does Cathy have enough money from the interest to pay the electricity bill? Explain your answer.

Solution

(i) €8·65 × 40 = €346

(ii) Gross pay = 100% = €346

$$1\% = \frac{346}{100}$$

$$\text{Gross tax} = 20\% = \frac{346 \times 20}{100} = €69\text{·}20.$$

(iii) Net tax = Gross tax − Tax credit
= €69·20 − €20 = €49·20

(iv) Amount Cathy is left with
= €346 − €49·20 = €296·80

(v) Principal = 100% = €1 650

$$1\% = \frac{1\,650}{100}$$

$$\text{Interest} = 4\text{·}5\% = \frac{1\,650}{100} \times 4\text{·}5 = €74\text{·}25$$

This question was awarded a total of 31 marks. Part **(vi)** was awarded 10 of those marks. Do not get tired when answering such a long question. Your best concentration is required on every part of every question.

(vi) 250 units @ 20 cents each = 250 × 0·20 = €50
Standing charge = €30
Total bill = €80

(vii) Interest = €74·25 } Cathy is short (€80 − €74·25) by €5·75. She does
    Bill = €80 } not have enough money to pay the bill from the interest.

17 Classroom-Based Assessments (CBAs)

aims

- ☐ To become familiar with the four elements of assessment for Junior Cycle mathematics
- ☐ To be familiar with the details of the Classroom-Based Assessment 1
- ☐ To be able to understand and apply the Problem-Solving Cycle
- ☐ To be familiar with the criteria of quality for assessment
- ☐ To understand the four descriptors for the CBA and the criteria associated with each descriptor
- ☐ To understand the steps involved in starting your investigation and examining a menu of suggestions for investigation
- ☐ To be familiar with the procedure involved with how to carry out a mathematical investigation
- ☐ To be able to use the checklist provided to ensure that you haven't missed any key elements in your investigation

Introduction

As mentioned in the Introduction chapter of this book, your assessment in Junior Cycle mathematics consists of four elements.

1. **Classroom-Based Assessment 1 (CBA 1)**

   This is a mathematical investigation and it is carried out during your second year of the three-year Junior Cycle. **CBA 1 is covered in this chapter.**

2. **Classroom-Based Assessment 2 (CBA 2)**

   This is a statistical investigation and it is carried out during your third year of the three-year Junior Cycle. **CBA 2 is covered in the** *Less Stress More Success Maths Book 2.*

3. **Assessment Task**

   This is a written assignment and it is carried out during your third year of the three-year Junior Cycle, after you have completed CBA 2.

4. **Written exam paper**

   This is a 2-hour written exam and it take place at the end of third year, with the rest of your written exams.

CBA 1: Mathematical Investigation

The investigation is an opportunity for you to show that you can apply mathematics to an area that interests you. Your teacher will give you a timetable and deadline for submitting your investigation.

The details of the investigation are as follows:

Format: A report may be presented in a wide range of formats.

Preparation: A student will, over a three-week period in second year, follow the Problem-Solving Cycle to investigate a mathematical problem.

The Problem-Solving Cycle is as follows:

1. Define a problem
2. Decompose it into manageable parts and/or simplify it using appropriate assumptions
3. Translate the problem to mathematics, if necessary
4. Engage with the problem and solve it, if possible
5. Interpret any findings in the context of the original problem

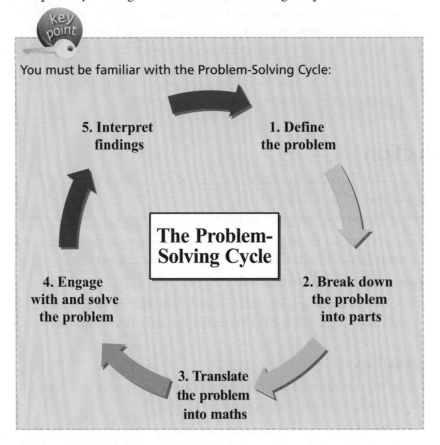

key point

You must be familiar with the Problem-Solving Cycle:

5. Interpret findings

1. Define the problem

The Problem-Solving Cycle

4. Engage with and solve the problem

2. Break down the problem into parts

3. Translate the problem into maths

CBA 1: Assessment criteria and four descriptors

The investigation is assessed by the class teacher. A student will be awarded one of the following categories of achievement:

- Yet to meet expectations
- In line with expectations
- Above expectations
- Exceptional

Assessment criteria

A good investigation should be clear and easily understood by one of your fellow classmates (peers) and self-explanatory all of the way through.

The criteria are split into four areas A, B, C and D:

A. Defining the problem statement

B. Finding a strategy or translating the problem to mathematics

C. Engaging with the mathematics to solve the problem

D. Interpreting and reporting

Linking the criteria with the four categories of achievement (descriptors)

A. Defining the problem statement

Criteria	Achievement
Uses a given problem statement and with guidance breaks the problem down into steps	Yet to achieve expectations
With guidance poses a problem statement, breaks the problem down into manageable steps and simplifies the problem by making assumptions, if appropriate	In line with expectations
With limited guidance poses a problem statement and clarifies/simplifies the problem by making reasonable assumptions, where appropriate	Above expectations
Poses a concise problem statement and clarifies and simplifies the problem by making justified assumptions, where appropriate	Exceptional

B. Finding a strategy or translating the problem to mathematics

Criteria	Achievement
Uses a given strategy	Yet to achieve expectations
Chooses an appropriate strategy to engage with the problem	In line with expectations
Justifies the use of a suitable strategy to engage with the problem and identifies any relevant variables	Above expectations
Develops an efficient justified strategy and evaluates progress towards a solution where appropriate; conjectures relationship between variables where appropriate	Exceptional

C. Engaging with the mathematics to solve the problem

Criteria	Achievement
Records some observations/data and follows some basic mathematical procedures	Yet to achieve expectations
Records observations/data and follows suitable mathematical procedures with minor errors; graphs and/or diagrams/words are used to provide insights into the problem and/or solution	In line with expectations
Records observations/data systematically, suitable mathematical procedures are followed, and accurate mathematical language, symbolic notation and visual representations are used; attempts are made to generalise any observed patterns in the solution/observation	Above expectations
Mathematical procedures are followed with a high level of precision, and a justified answer is achieved; solution/observations are generalised and extended to other situations where appropriate	Exceptional

D. Interpreting and reporting

Criteria	Achievement
Comments on any solution	Yet to achieve expectations
Comments on the reasonableness of the solution where appropriate and makes a concrete connection to the original question, uses everyday familiar language to communicate ideas	In line with expectations
Checks reasonableness of solution and revisits assumptions and/or strategy to iterate the process, if necessary, uses formal mathematical language to communicate ideas and identifies what worked well and what could be improved	Above expectations
Deductive arguments used and precise mathematical language and symbolic notation used to consolidate mathematical thinking and justify decisions and solutions; strengths and/or weaknesses in the mathematical representation/solution strategy are identified	Exceptional

Academic honesty

Academic honesty means that your work is based on your own original ideas and not copied from other people. However, you may draw on the work and ideas of others, but this must be acknowledged. This would be put into a reference list at the end of your investigation, known as a bibliography. In addition, you should use your own language and expression.

Record-keeping

Throughout the investigation, keep a journal, either on paper or online. This journal will also help you to demonstrate academic honesty. The journal will be of great assistance in focusing your efforts when writing your CBA 1 investigation.

- Make notes of any websites or books you use.
- You are encouraged to use a variety of support materials and present your work in a variety of formats.
- Keep a record of your actions so you can show your teacher how much time you are spending on your investigation.
- Remember to follow your teacher's advice and meet your CBA 1 timetable.
- The teacher is there to facilitate you, so do not be afraid to ask for guidance. The more focused your questions are, the better guidance your teacher can give you.

Evidence of learning

The following evidence is required

- A report
- Student research records

You must report your research and findings in a format of your choice. The report can be completed at the end of the investigation. If a typed or hand-written report is the format of choice, the total length of the report would typically be in the 400–600 words range (excluding tables, graphs, reference list and research records), but this should not be regarded as a rigid requirement.

Choosing a topic

You should choose a topic that you are interested in, because then you will be inclined to put more effort into the project. In addition, you will enjoy working on your project and this will shine through. You should discuss the topic with your teacher before you put too much time and effort into it, in case your idea is not in line with what a mathematical investigation should be.

If you cannot think of a topic yourself, then you can ask your teacher for help in coming up with a topic to investigate. Below are some ideas that might help you to come up with an investigation of your own.

Suggestions for investigation, with ideas to consider:

- Investigating the cost of a family weekend in a foreign city
  - o Destination
  - o Transportation
  - o Hotel
  - o Currency exchange
  - o Activities
- Garden design
  - o Size, shape and dimensions of garden
  - o Features: flower bed/pond/trees/patio
  - o Draw a sketch
  - o Work out costs
- Bedroom makeover
  - o Carpet/wooden floor
  - o Walls painted or wallpapered
  - o Furniture – bed/desk/wardrobe
  - o Decoration
  - o Work out costs
- Best placement of security sensors in different shaped rooms
  - o Radius of detection on the average sensor
  - o Best placement in a rectangular room/square room/L-shaped room
- An environmental investigation, for example, glass recycling
  - o Mass of glass per bottle bank
  - o How often the bank is emptied
  - o Average mass of glass recycled per household

- Traffic study at an airport or local train station
  - o Number of cars in and out daily
  - o Number of foot passengers passing through
  - o Number of airplanes/trains arriving and departing daily
  - o Peak times?
- Budgeting for a 'Debs ball' for a couple
  - o Cost of dress/suit hire
  - o Beauty treatments – tan, nails, makeup, haircuts
  - o Transport to and from the venue
  - o Spending money
- Cost of installing solar panels in a house and expected savings in energy and environmental costs
  - o Cost of annual electricity bill
  - o Cost of installing solar panels
  - o Amount of energy generated
  - o Annual savings
- Public transport costs and car usage: A personal comparison
  - o Annual cost of running a car – insurance, tax, depreciation
  - o Petrol costs
  - o Bus/train/taxi use for equivalent journeys
- Mapping the path of a diver jumping from a board into water
  - o Video record a diver/observe a video
  - o Using a point of reference, note down the height of the diver after every 0·1 of a second.
  - o Graph results. Observe shape
- Investigate the potential profit that can be made from buying ingredients and baking cupcakes for a school cake sale
  - o How many cupcakes will you make?
  - o Ingredients needed and cost of same
  - o Selling price of cupcakes
  - o Profit?
- Using a map of your local area, design a 10 km fun-run route. Use average speeds of walkers and runners to work out how long the route should be closed for, to allow the run to take place
  - o Look at a map of the local area and look at different options for a route
  - o One single route or a 5 km route that is done twice?
  - o Is there a route that will cause least disruption? Park/road/country lanes?

- Investigate which electricity energy provider is offering the best deal at the moment, for an average family home
    - Average annual usage of electricity
    - Compare cost of electricity from various suppliers
- Investigate the cost of pet ownership
    - Initial cost of getting a pet
    - Equipment (bed/toys/fish tank)
    - Annual cost of food and treats
    - Vet visits
    - Kennelling/cattery costs while on holiday
- Investigate fitness programmes for muscle building or calorie burning
    - Compare various workout routines – aerobics/cardio/weight-lifting
    - Time spent on a regime
- Investigate the breakdown of how teenagers spend their money
    - Sources of income – pocket money/part-time job/gifts
    - Breakdown of expenditure

Getting started

Once you have chosen your investigation, the next step is to do some research. The purpose of this research is to determine the suitability of your investigation. Do not limit your research to the internet. Your local or school library will have books on mathematics that are interesting and may be useful.

The following questions may help you decide if your chosen investigation is suitable:

- What area of mathematics are contained in my investigation?
- Can I understand and use the mathematics required?
- Can I define a precise problem statement related to this topic?
- Am I totally familiar with the problem-solving cycle?
- Have I clearly defined the problem statement?
- How can I show the work I did, as part of my investigation?
- Can I limit my work to the 400–600 word range report (excluding tables, graphs, reference list, bibliography and research records) if I choose this investigation?

If your original investigation is not suitable, has your research suggested another, better investigation? Otherwise, could you either narrow down or widen out your investigation to make it suitable?

Once you think you have a workable investigation, then you must start into the Problem-Solving Cycle by carrying out the following steps:

    A. Define the problem
    B. Translate the problem to mathematics
    C. Engage with the mathematics to solve the problem
    D. Interpret and report your findings

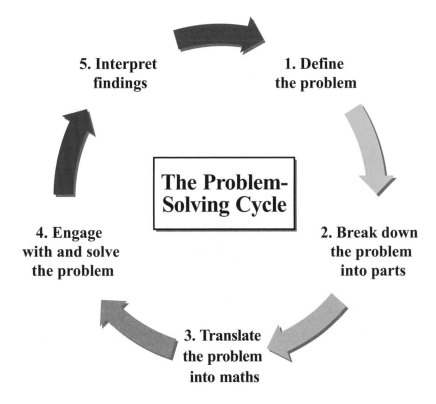

Now you are ready to start writing your investigation in detail.

Remember that your peers (fellow students) should be able to read and understand your investigation.

The following table, designed to support teachers in giving feedback to their students, will help you when carrying out each step of your investigation.

Area of Activity	Questions to focus on during formative feedback	Vocabulary to build
Defining the problem	What is the big problem that you are trying to investigate/solve? Does it have more than one possible answer?	Open-ended problem Constraints
Defining the problem	What is the specific problem your mathematical representation is going to investigate/solve? What elements are you going to focus on during your investigation?	Specific, focus
Translating to mathematics (if necessary)	What ideas did you think about that you decided not to try?	Eliminate, prioritise
Translating to mathematics (if necessary)	What have you assumed in order to investigate/solve the problem? Why did you make these choices?	Assumptions
Translating to mathematics (if necessary)	What qualities are important? Which ones change and which ones stay the same?	Variables
Engaging with the problem and solving it if possible	Where did you find the numbers that you used?	Research
Engaging with the problem and solving it if possible	What pictures, diagrams or graphs might help people understand your information, mathematical representation and results?	Diagrams, graphs, tables
Engaging with the problem and solving it if possible	What mathematical ideas did you use to describe the situation and solve your problem?	Mathematical ideas
Interpreting the solution	How do you know that your calculations are correct? Did you remember to use units €, cm, etc.?	Calculation, unit

Area of Activity	Questions to focus on during formative feedback	Vocabulary to build
Interpreting the solution	When does your mathematical representation work? When do you need to be careful because it might not?	Limitations
Interpreting the solution	How do you know that you have a good useful mathematical representation? Why does your representation make sense?	Testing, validation
Interpreting the solution	Could you do anything to make your mathematical representation better or more accurate?	Improvement, iteration
Communicating/ Reporting results	Explain your representation in words and mathematical notation	Mathematical notation
Communicating/ Reporting results	How did each of your teammates help?	Collaboration
Communicating/ Reporting results	What are the most important things for your audience to understand about your mathematical representation and/or solution?	Audience

Source www.ncca.ie

Mind map for CBA

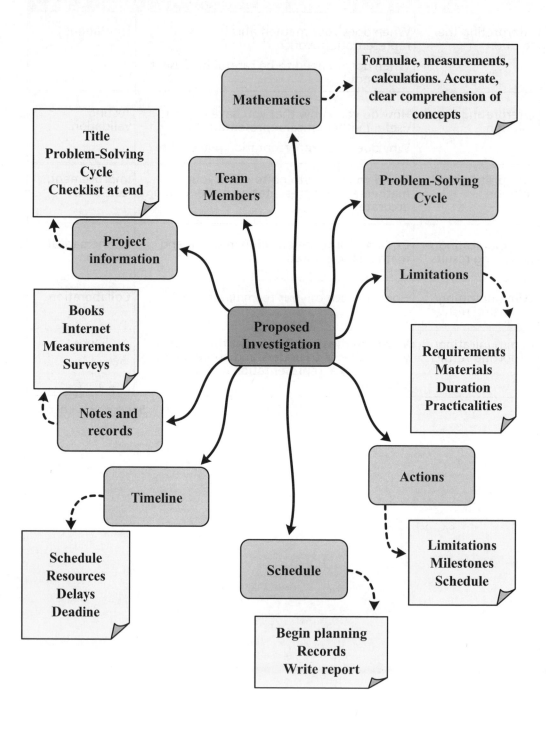

Classroom-Based Assessment Investigation Checklist

Before completing your CBA, go through the following checklist and make sure that you have completed each task.

Activity	Completed?
Does your project have a front cover with the project title and your name?	
Have you started clearly what you are going to do?	
Have you explained how you are going to do it?	
Have you explained what mathematical methods you will use and why?	
Did you do everything you said you would do?	
Have you collected data or generated measurements or information?	
Is your raw data included in the project or in the appendix, at the end?	
Is your data relevant?	
Is your data sufficient in quantity? Have you enough data?	
Do you have quality data?	
Is your data ready to use immediately, or do you need to do some work on it first?	
Have you performed relevant mathematical processes?	
Are these processes correct?	
Does the project contain only correct notation?	
Does the project contain only correct terminology?	
Is your project laid out in a logical manner?	
Are your diagrams and tables of good clear quality?	
Have you commented on your results?	
Are your comments consistent with your analysis?	
Have you commented thoroughly on everything that you have done?	
Have you commented on validity?	
Do you have an appendix, if one is needed?	
Do you have a bibliography?	